Become an Approved Driving Instructor

and set up your own driving school

Become an
Approved
Driving
Instructor

and set up your own driving school

Colin Crane & Paul Pearson

how tobooks

Published by How To Books Ltd,
Spring Hill House, Spring Hill Road,
Begbroke, Oxford OX5 1RX
Tel: (01865) 375794. Fax: (01865) 379162
info@howtobooks.co.uk
www.howtobooks.co.uk

How To Books greatly reduce the carbon footprint of their books by sourcing
their typesetting and printing in the UK.

British Library Cataloguing in Publication Data
A catalogue record for this book is available from the British Library

ISBN: 978 1 84528 348 3

Cover design by Baseline Arts, Oxford
Produced for How To Books by Deer Park Productions, Tavistock
Typeset by Pantek Arts Ltd, Maidstone
Printed and bound by Cromwell Press Group, Trowbridge, Wiltshire

NOTE: The material contained in this book is set out in good faith for general
guidance and no liability can be accepted for the loss or expense incurred as a
result of relying in particular circumstances on statements made in the book.
The laws and regulations are complex and liable to change, and readers should
check the current position with the relevant authorities before making
personal arrangements.

Contents

About the authors

The authors are business partners who jointly own a driving school website that sells top-quality materials to instructors and trainers. They also operate their own individual and successful driving schools in the South of England.

Colin Crane first started his working career as a teacher and took early retirement after 29 years as a head teacher, having fulfilled his ambition to have his own school built to his own design and specifications and operating a unique style of teaching within it. In the latter years of his teaching he retrained as a driving instructor and quite quickly built up a large driving school (covering four counties) which he later sold. He now operates another very successful driving school with a constant, full diary. He also undertakes ADI training and is a RoSPA (Gold) advanced driver and tutor.

Paul Pearson came to the driving training industry from the fire service. During his 25 years as an operational fire-fighter, he also carried out the duties of a fire service instructor, where he gained valuable experience in instructing and running courses and in setting fire service exams. As he had enjoyed instructing it seemed only natural, on retirement from the service, to become an ADI. After working for a local driving school for 12 months he decided to start his own driving school, which, over the years, has gone from strength to strength.

Several years ago Colin and Paul collaborated to form a joint website with the philosophy of producing good-value training and business aids that ADIs and PDIs would find extremely valuable. The first of these products was graphic briefings.

Graphic Briefings have been developed over the years, resulting in a set of training aids for both trainees and qualified instructors to use. Logbooks followed. After this, Colin and Paul realised that there was another gap in the market. It occurred to them both that the one thing they would have dearly loved in their early days was a no-nonsense guide – not only on how to become an ADI but also on how to go about setting up your own driving school. This would have helped to avoid time-consuming and frustrating pitfalls and would have kept their training and other costs to a minimum. From this, this book evolved.

Preface

While we were exploring the idea of becoming driving instructors and throughout our training and the setting up of our own driving schools, nowhere could we find anything to help us do this or to evade the numerous pitfalls we fell into. Yes, we have learnt a great deal in the past 12 years, and the purpose of this book – along with all the other products we have designed and made within our joint driving-school businesses – is to help others to decide on the best course of action for them and to run smooth and successful businesses.

So this book is for those who are considering becoming a driving instructor, before they give up their current employment; for those who are seeking an approved driving instructor (ADI) training course; for those who are already on such a course (and perhaps who now wish they had read this book first); for those coming to the end of their course or who have just qualified and who want to know the pros and cons of working for another driving school or of setting up their own driving school; or, indeed, for those who are considering expanding their school perhaps to that of a regional driving school.

When considering any of the above, it is most important that you understand fully the implications of this business, the impact it may have on your family and social life and the stresses and strains of running your own business. Therefore spend as much time as necessary to decide whether this business is for you; otherwise you could spend many thousands of pounds to no avail.

We do not suggest that the content of this book guarantees a successful business as each reader may take on board some of the points made and may discard others in personalising their own, unique driving school. But reading this may help the process and may help you to avoid some of the mistakes we made.

Good luck!

Colin Crane

Paul Pearson

Introduction

Whether you are tentatively exploring this career opportunity, are a trainee or are an approved driving instructor (ADI) considering setting up your own driving school or working for a driving school, we believe you will find the information in this book to be essential reading. Not only will it help you avoid time-consuming pitfalls but it could also help you save thousands of pounds.

Purchasing this book has shown your commitment to finding out more about this profession – yes, profession! We believe that, if you have taken the time, trouble and expense to have studied in great depth and passed the increasingly difficult stages of the Driving Standards Agency tests, then you can quite rightly call it a profession. You will have gained the skills necessary to teach people of all walks of life, from the age of 17 to 70, to master the difficult process of learning to drive well in the ever-demanding environments of Britain's roads.

To readers who are exploring the idea of becoming a driving instructor, we strongly recommend you read carefully through Chapter 1 and then assess more fully the financial and time commitments you will have to make. If and when you decide that being an ADI is for you, we suggest you read the entire book as each chapter contains very valuable advice.

Throughout this book you will notice that certain points are repeated. This is deliberate in order to reinforce these very important aspects. You will find explanations of industry abbreviations and information on website addresses, etc., in the appendices.

Note: any purchasing suggestions or recommendations we make in this book are based on personal experience and preferences only. We receive no commission from such sources. The sole purpose of this book is to help our readers to the best of our ability.

Disclaimer

Although the authors have tried to make the content as accurate as possible, they cannot be held responsible for any inaccuracies found post-publication. Rules and regulations may change. Readers should consult the organisations directly (e.g. the DSA) via their websites to check the information given in this book.

The driving training profession is changing all the time and the DSA introduce new procedures on a fairly regular basis. To keep up with any news please log onto the DS Pro website.

1

Becoming an approved driving instructor

❝ *This chapter will help you to discover whether you are suited to becoming a driving instructor and what is involved.* ❞

Are you sure you want to become an approved driving instructor (ADI)?

The first step is to find out whether you will make a good driving instructor and whether this career is for you. Many readers will have done their home-work and will know exactly what becoming a driving instructor involves. Others may not have looked at it fully and, indeed, this may be one of the reasons they have purchased this book. It is not our intention to deter anyone from becoming a driving instructor but to help you to make a realistic and well informed decision about what to expect from the driver training industry.

For a multitude of reasons, many people have looked around and decided that being a driving instructor is the career for them. Some may tell themselves that it surely cannot be that difficult to teach people to drive. They may also believe that driving instructors get a very good income and that, if they work under a franchise agreement, they get a car as well. Let us explore these perceptions further.

How difficult can it be?

If teaching people of all walks of life, ages and abilities was easy, driving instructors would be almost non-existent as families and friends would cheer-fully take on the task. Also, before you can teach people to drive for financial gain as a fully qualified Driving Standards Agency approved driving instructor (DSA ADI – car), you will have to pass three increasingly difficult DSA exams. The drop-out rate for people who decide part way through the course that being an ADI is not for them is depressingly high. The failure rate for the three ADI tests is approximately 50% for Part 1, 55% for Part 2 and 72% for Part 3. This book has been written in part to help you avoid making these time-consuming and very costly mistakes.

A good income?

Your income will be at the mercy of a variety of factors and may fluctuate over the year. You will encounter extra costs that will be a drain on your income. Your first major cost will be your training fees, which may be thousands of pounds.

A free car?

If you work under a franchise, you may well get a car, but it certainly will not be free. You will be paying for it one way or another as franchise companies do not hold charity status.

The reality of being an ADI

If you are seriously considering becoming a driving instructor, now is the time to look at things objectively. Becoming a driving instructor will take a lot of your time and a lot of your money. You must make sure that you are making the right decision, *now*.

For a moment we ask that you put to one side any rosy images you may have of earning thousands of pounds a month while effortlessly supervising the driving of your new school car through the sun-dappled lanes. Step out from the dream, look closely at the questions below and answer them honestly. (Please note that, for brevity, the comments following the questions cover just a few of the points. To find out more, please refer to the appropriate chapters of this book.)

Being a self-employed ADI

Being self-employed has its advantages and disadvantages. For example, although you can have flexible working hours you may also work what most people would consider to be unsociable hours. Although you will be 'your own boss', you will not have the benefits and piece of mind of sick pay, paid holidays or company pension schemes. You will not even have the guarantee of a consistent and steady income. Very many ADIs have to work part time due to having insufficient clients. If you have a large mortgage or other financial commitments you should consider this very carefully. Look closely at the appropriate chapters of this book to find out more.

Driving for a living as an ADI

Unless you have driven for a living, you may not fully appreciate what it feels like to be sat in a car for up to nine hours a day. You will not even be driving for most of that time – your client will. It will not be, and should not be, as relaxing as you might think.

Working in a one-to-one situation

You may enjoy socialising on a one-to-one basis but being in close proximity to someone you may not even like or who may also have personal hygiene problems is a totally different matter.

Are you fit for the job?

You may think that fitness is probably not a problem for a sedentary job like giving driving instruction. But there are fitness issues. Your back has to be able to withstand being in one position for long periods. You should also be mentally fit to withstand the rigours of having learners drive you through potentially dangerous situations, possibly many times a day. If you have any doubts about your general health you should visit your GP and ask for advice before you proceed any further.

Working alongside people of different cultures, social backgrounds and ages

Clients from different cultures may not be able to speak English very well, if at all. They may have a totally different way of looking at problem-solving, which can lead to difficulties. Generally your clients:

☐ will have differing levels of aptitude and ability;

☐ may not even want to learn to drive; and

☐ may have a poor attitude towards life in general or to driving – or even towards you, in particular.

Your clients may also have:

☐ poor co-ordination;

☐ poor retention of information;

☐ learning difficulties; and/or

☐ physical difficulties.

Then, of course, you will have those who think they know it all because they have seen their parents drive or talked to their friends and concluded that it must be simple. Some may think that, because they were once at test standard (supposedly) ten years ago, they only need a couple of top-up lessons before taking their test. What about a timid 17-year-old who cannot converse, who cannot reverse and who starts to cry every time something goes wrong?

The skills and qualities required to be an ADI

Ask yourself the following questions to find out if you have the skills and qualities to be an ADI:

□ Are you able to communicate with others in a clear and logical manner?

□ Are you blessed with endless patience and understanding?

□ Will you be able to correct mistakes in a good-humoured way even when your client seems intent on damaging your car or causing an accident?

□ Will you be able to remain tolerant when your client makes the same simple error many, many times?

□ Are you a good listener?

□ Do you have good powers of observation?

□ Will you have the stamina and commitment to be able to remain as enthusiastic at 8.30 p.m. as you were at 8.30 a.m.?

Your finances and support

Again, ask yourself the following questions to find out about your finances and other forms of support:

□ Will you be able to study intensively at home over a period of months?

□ Do you have the finances and time to undertake the training necessary to complete the course?

□ If you have a family, will they be supportive?

□ What if you fail the last test for the third and final time after all the time and money spent?

□ When you have (hopefully) passed the test will your present car be suitable for driving lessons or will you need to spend even more money on a new(er) car – and, if so, will that money be available?

Conditions set by the Driving Standards Agency

In accordance with the DSA's regulations, before becoming a DSA ADI and registered as such, each trainee must:

☐ hold a full British or Northern Ireland unrestricted car-driving licence;

☐ have held this for a total of at least four out of the past six years prior to entering the register after qualifying (a foreign driving licence, an automatic-car driving licence or a provisional licence held after passing the driving test all count towards the four years);

☐ not have been disqualified from driving at any time in the four years prior to being entered on the ADI register;

☐ be able to read a car number plate at a distance of 27.5 m (90 ft) where the letters are 79.4 mm (⅜ inch) tall, with the help of spectacles or contact lenses, if worn;

☐ be a fit and proper person and clear the criminal records check to have their name entered in the register. All convictions, including motoring offences still in force (i.e. not 'spent' under the Rehabilitation of Offenders Act 1974), will be taken into account when the DSA Registrar assesses a person's suitability to be entered in the register. We suggest you complete the Disclosure Application Form from the Criminal Records Bureau and send this off well before booking your Part 1 test, as it can take about two months to process. Your test cannot be booked until you receive clearance from the bureau. This form should come in the ADI 14 pack;

☐ pass the register's three qualifying exams; and

☐ be aware that they cannot accompany a person unless they have held a full UK driving licence for three years and that they must be aged 21 or more (a foreign full licence will count towards this three-year period but it must be a foreign licence that is accepted under the 'exchange' scheme – see section 4 of the DVLA pamphlet D100).

If you have answered all the questions satisfactorily, fulfilling all the above conditions, and you still want to be a driving instructor, then now is the time to find out about the three tests and training courses involved.

The three qualifying ADI tests

Aims and objectives

The aim now is to pass all three increasingly difficult tests. They must be done in this order and, when you have passed each one, the examiner will provide you with the form to complete regarding the next test.

ADI Part 1: the written test

This is considered by most to be the easiest test. The Part 1 test comprises:

1. test paper; and

2. hazard perception.

Test paper

The first part of the Part 1 test is a test paper containing 100 questions in a multiple-choice answer format using a touch-screen computer and mouse. For example:

Q. Anti-lock braking system allows the driver to:

A. a) apply the brakes and steer at the same time

   b) accelerate without skidding

   c) brake without fear of skidding

   d) corner faster than cars without ABS

The 100 questions are divided into four bands:

1. Road procedure.

2. Traffic signs and signals, car control, pedestrians and mechanical knowledge.

3. The driving test, disabilities and the law.

4. Publications and instructional technique.

Test paper pass mark

The pass mark is 85% but you must reach a minimum of 80% (20 out of 25) in each of the four bands. This test must be completed in 90 minutes.

Hazard perception

After the test paper you have up to three minutes before taking the second part of the theory test.

The second part of this test requires you to watch 14 video clips of actual driving situations from the perspective of the driver and to respond by clicking the computer mouse when you see a hazardous situation ahead. To achieve a high score, you need to respond to the developing hazards. The maximum you can achieve per clip is five points in the unseen scoring window.

Hazard perception pass mark

You will be given your result once you have left the room. Check the DSA website (see Appendix 1) to find the current test fee and pass mark.

ADI Part 2: the driving technique test

Your driving licence

You are required to present your driving licence (old style plus your passport or both parts of the new photo-style licence) together with the letter for this test from the DSA. If you intend becoming an ADI and if you do not have a new-style licence or a passport, then you should now consider applying for a new-style licence.

The vehicle

You are required to undertake the test in a vehicle that is properly taxed and insured. This vehicle:

☐ must be a saloon car or a hatchback/estate car in good working condition without a space-saver tyre on any of the four wheels, with functioning seat belts and head restraint on both front seats;

☐ must have a manual transmission, right-hand steering and an adjustable interior, rear-view mirror for use by the examiner; and

☐ must not display 'L' plates.

The Part 2 test comprises:

1. an eyesight test;

2. safety questions; and

3. driving technique.

Eyesight test

The conditions of the eyesight test were described earlier.

Safety questions

The safety questions require you successfully to:

☐ describe how to perform a check on the condition and safety of three of the vehicle's components; and

☐ demonstrate an actual check on the condition of another two components.

Driving technique

The driving test requires you to undertake an advanced-style drive to a very high standard within the following areas:

☐ Expert handling of the controls.

☐ Use of correct road procedure.

☐ Anticipation of the actions of other road users and the taking of appropriate action where necessary.

☐ Sound judgement of distance, speed and timing.

☐ Consideration for the convenience and safety of other road users.

The routes will include fast-moving traffic and a range of road and traffic conditions on urban and rural roads, including a dual carriageway/motorway.

You will also be required to demonstrate:

☐ three reversing manoeuvres;

☐ moving off straight or at an angle;

☐ turning corners accurately and without any unnecessary hesitation;

☐ overtaking, meeting or crossing the path of other vehicles; and

☐ an emergency stop.

The Part 2 test lasts about an hour. You will be given the result of your test by the examiner at its conclusion.

After passing the tests

Once you have passed the Part 2 test you have two courses of action available to you before taking the Part 3 test. You can take further instruction for the Part 3 and apply for the test when you think you are ready, or you could consider using the Trainee Licence Scheme where you must undertake the regulatory, minimum, 40 hours' Part 3 training with a qualified instructor/trainer. Then you may apply for a trainee licence that is valid for six months. Following this you will be able to work in association with a driving school/ADI under supervision and/or to receive further training supported by your trainer (as required under the DSA trainee licence regulations) while receiving tuition fees.

Part 3: the instructional ability test

This is considered by nearly everyone to be the hardest test. You must take your driving licence with you to the test.

Format of the Part 3 test

The test is in two phases, each lasting 30 minutes. During each phase you will be asked to give instruction on one of 12 listed exercises. You must pass both phases.

Objectives of the Part 3 test

The object of this test is for the examiner to assess the quality of your instruction and your ability to pass on your knowledge of driving to your clients. You will be expected to give driving instruction to the examiner, who will be role playing as a beginner or someone with limited driving knowledge and, finally, as someone who is at about test standard.

Being assessed

You will be assessed regarding your:

☐ manner, clarity, adequacy and correctness of instruction given;

☐ observation, analysis and correction of faults committed by your client; and

☐ general manner.

What is assessed is the relevance of the instruction for your client's ability and to the particular road conditions on the day of the test. You will be expected to maintain control of the lesson, to be patient and tactful and to give encouragement to your client at all times.

The test exercises

The examiner will select one of the following exercises for each part of the test:

☐ Safety precautions on entering the car and an explanation of the car's main controls.

☐ Moving off and making normal stops.

☐ Reversing into a limited opening to the left or right.

☐ Turning in the road.

☐ Reverse/parallel parking, either behind a vehicle or into a bay.

☐ The use of mirrors and how to undertake an emergency stop.

☐ Approaching and turning corners.

☐ Judgement of speed, making progress and general road positioning.

☐ Dealing with road junctions (emerging).

☐ Dealing with crossroads.

☐ Dealing with pedestrian crossings and giving correct signals in a clear and unmistakable manner.

☐ Overtaking, meeting and crossing the path of other road users, allowing adequate clearance.

The examiner's role play

The examiner will adopt the role of:

☐ a novice driver; or

☐ an elementary standard driver; and then

☐ Someone who is almost at test standard but who is still making errors. Or it may be someone who has been disqualified from driving and who now has a new provisional licence and needs to pass their test, with you trying to eliminate their bad driving habits. They are not likely to be pleased with you teaching them how to drive 'properly'!

Whatever role they play, you must forget that they are your examiner and not assume that they can drive or will comply with your instructions. This is what many trainees find difficult.

(More in-depth information about these three tests can be found in Chapter 3.)

Training for the tests

Consider carefully whether you actually need to do a course for the Part 1 test. Many people do this exam without any help from a driving school – which is obviously a lot cheaper. You can obtain the full question bank from the DSA and then just study at home. On the other hand some people prefer to do a professional Part 1 course because:

    ☐ it gives them an added impetus;

    ☐ they receive help from people who know what's required; and

    ☐ it gives them the opportunity to see and question how the driver-training industry works.

Training courses

ADI training schools have differing ways of teaching trainee driving instructors. The syllabus laid out below is from the Driving School Pro ADI training schools. Although this programme may exceed that of other establishments, it will give you some idea of what you should expect.

(An example of the resource material used on the Driving School Pro course can be found in Appendix 2.)

ADI Part 1 course

You will need to set aside many hours of study time to read and learn the material required. We advise that you do not read each book from cover to cover; rather, read relevant material in the books on the topics shown below.

It is also advisable to study without distractions for periods of about an hour at a time, giving yourself a break before undertaking the next study session. Doing this at the end of a working day is not ideal.

Only when you believe you are knowledgeable in all aspects of the course content should you begin to answer the questions in the DSA Theory Test

Bank, which should either come with your ADI 14 pack.

As you realise the mistakes you make, write them down (and check to see whether they fall into one or more categories – bands) on a separate sheet. It is these you will need to learn, having first done some additional background reading.

When satisfied that you are ready, book your theory test by telephone or via the internet. You cannot book it at the local theory test centre.

Training syllabus for Part 1
The following is the syllabus for Part 1:

1. Background information about the DSA and the driver training industry.

2. Qualifying as, and the grading of, ADIs.

3. The qualities and characteristics expected from ADIs.

4. An explanation of the Part 1 examination, including:

   □ the 'L' driving test;

   □ the driving test report form;

   □ the Motor Vehicles (Driving Licences) Regulations;

   □ the theory and practice of learning, teaching and assessment; and

   □ the hazard perception test.

Note: the maximum number of attempts allowed to pass this test is unlimited (at present).

ADI Part 2 course
This aspect of the course incorporates driving to the standard described in the DSA's *Driving Manual*. This is *not* just a slightly more difficult 'L' test. A drive of an advanced nature is required showing a thorough knowledge of the principles of good driving and road safety, as well as driving with skill and confidence.

Even though you may have been driving for many years, bad habits develop. Not only does this need to be eliminated or modified but also new driving techniques may need to be developed until you drive to a consistently high standard as the norm. The standard required may be higher than that of some advanced driving organisations.

Some of the areas of driving that usually need attention are:

☐ attitude to other drivers;

☐ steering technique;

☐ gear changing;

☐ using all mirrors effectively;

☐ planning to make effective use of the accelerator and brakes;

☐ planning to avoid adding to the hazards ahead; and

☐ emerging from junctions.

Training syllabus for Part 2

The following is the syllabus for Part 2:

1. Driving technique, car control, road procedure, hazard recognition/ proper response, dealing safely with other road users and pedestrians and the use of safety equipment.

2. Vehicle suitability.

3. Knowledge of basic car mechanics and car design applicable to giving driving instruction.

4. The Part 2 test, including:

☐ instructional techniques, fault assessment and lesson planning;

☐ drivers with disabilities and simple vehicle adaptations; and

☐ licensed trainees.

Note: the maximum number of attempts allowed to pass this test is three (at present).

Further areas that are discussed include the following:

☐ Choices/decisions. Should you later join an established driving school or set up on your own?

☐ The resource material that will be used on the course.

☐ Answering any driving-related questions the trainee may wish to ask.

ADI Part 3 course

Most people find the Part 3 course and the Part 3 test the most difficult. The Part 3 course is the lengthiest and, if the trainee wishes to give paid instruction using a trainee licence, then they must also undertake the mandatory 40 hours compulsory training. The trainee licence can be very useful. It licenses the trainee to give driving instruction to the general public and to receive a fee for doing so. More information on the trainee licence can be found below.

On the Part 3 course you will spend many hours with your trainer, not only learning how to teach people to drive but also how to cope with the situations the examiner is going to present to you on the test day. You will most likely find that trying to control your 'learner' (i.e. your trainer in role play) is frustratingly difficult at first. You may consider that your trainer is being outlandishly awkward but you will find that, once you have passed your Part 3, the world is full of people wishing to learn to drive who sometimes seem to be just like that.

Training syllabus for Part 3

The following is the syllabus for Part 3:

1. Observing lesson topics being given by an instructor 'live' to a real client, as can be arranged. This will occur at various times throughout the course.

2. Having your trainer deliver each lesson briefing to you as if you were the learner driver client.

3. Returning the briefing to your trainer or trainee colleague, as if they were your client, the following day.

4. Observing your trainee colleague giving instruction.

5. Continuing such practices until your trainer is satisfied with the standard you have reached.

6. Receiving a set of full Graphic Briefings (see Appendix 2, as Graphic Briefings are available to purchase from Driving School Pro).

7. Receiving a set of lesson briefing notes.

At the end of each lesson you will receive a verbal debriefing. At the end of each topic practised, you will receive a written report showing your strengths and weaknesses. This will help you to realise any further practices necessary before taking your Part 3 test.

The trainee licence

Once you have passed the second part of the ADI qualification process and have shown that you have completed 40 hours of instructional training, you may apply for a trainee licence. This helps you to gain experience – instructing clients to drive while legally being able to take payment for this. You will be issued with a pink, trainee driving instructor (car) licence to place inside the windscreen of your car (the qualified licence is green).

Note : If you opt to work under a trainee licence, it is obligatory that you receive 20 hours' additional training or supervision during the licence period (up to six months). This has to be certificated in order for you to take your part 3 test (see the DSA regulations at the DSA website).

You should not consider this to be your sole means of income as you may not pass the final test.

This licence is issued for a period of six months in order for you to gain practical experience in preparation for the Part 3 test. Unless there are exceptional circumstances that the Registrar agrees to, you are only granted this licence for one six-month period.

Applying for a trainee licence

If you apply for a trainee licence, you must:

☐ hold and have held a full UK or European (EU or EEA) car driving licence for a total of at least four years out of the past six years, up to the date of application;

☐ not have been disqualified from driving at anytime in the four years up to the date of application;

☐ be a fit and proper person. This now includes a criminal records check on you;

☐ have passed the theory part and the practical part of the qualifying examinations;

☐ be eligible to take the test of ability to instruct; and

☐ not have passed the theory test more than two years before the date of your application.

Trainee licence application form

The application form for a trainee licence can be obtained from the examiner who passes you on your driving ability test (Part 2 test).

Conditions for the trainee licence

Apart from meeting the above criteria, the licence will only be granted if you meet the following conditions:

☐ You are authorised to give instruction for the driving school whose address is shown on the licence.

☐ There must be at least one ADI working at the supervisor's address for every trainee licence holder employed there.

☐ You must receive 40 hours' practical training from a qualified ADI. It is your responsibility to make sure that you receive training in each of the specified subjects.

☐ You must not advertise yourself as a fully qualified instructor.

☐ you must abide by *one* of the following conditions. You must receive:

   ☐ supervision for 20% of all lessons you give from your sponsoring ADI. A record of all lessons given, along with the supervision received, must be kept on the form ADI 21S, which will be issued with the licence. This must be signed by you and your ADI and must be returned to the DSA as soon as the licence expires; or

   ☐ a minimum additional 20 hours of training. This extra training must take place within the first three months of receiving the licence or before you take your first attempt at Part 3, whichever is the soonest. A record of this training must be kept on the form ADI 21AT and must be sent to the DSA before the end of the three-month period or presented to the examiner conducting the Part 3 test, whichever is the earliest. At least 25% of the training will have to be practical.

Displaying the trainee licence

When instruction is being given to your clients, the trainee licence must be displayed in the bottom left-hand corner of the front windscreen. The use of the licence is your own responsibility. No refunds will be given for any period when the licence is not used.

If you cannot make full use of your licence and you have to stop giving tuition, you should return it immediately to the issuing office. If your trainee licence is lost or stolen you should report it to the police and to the DSA straightaway.

You can find out about the trainee licence and any new rules, by logging on to the DSA website.

Note:

☐ Of all those who begin the course, only about 20% succeed in qualifying. Therefore you are advised not to give up your main means of income until you are fully qualified.

☐ At the moment in the industry, there is an ongoing discussion as to whether the trainee licence should be dispensed with or changed in some way. This may mean that this facility may not be available at some time in the future, or in its present format.

2
Choosing your trainer

In this chapter we offer advice on what to look for when deciding which training school to use and warn of the many pitfalls you should be aware of.

Plan of action

Now that you have all the background information, it is time for you to consider taking an ADI training course – but be very careful. Many people have lived to regret the day they signed the contract too quickly and before they had considered all the conditions.

Which trainer do you go to?

Find out who delivers these courses in your area. Contact them by telephone to make an appointment to discuss matters. You will be well aware that, in any business, some are good and some not so good. The driving industry is no exception. There will be many honest people just trying to give good value for money – and there will be others. Beware!

We know that our readers, apart from having a mutual interest in the driver training industry, will differ considerably from one another. Because they may have a background that involves business meetings, a few will relish the thought of meeting the driving school proprietor. Others may be less comfortable with such a situation. All we can suggest is that you remember what this is all about. It is about *your* career and *your* money. As they will want your money, you have the advantage. They want your custom. Do not commit yourself yet. Explore other training establishments first.

Try to be strong willed

Remember that this is a business meeting rather than a cosy cup of tea with a friend. Do not try to be too friendly. Be alert. Do not be afraid to ask specific questions from your list (see below). Do not be diverted by a salesperson's over-active imagination that is possibly painting unrealistic pictures of your future as an ADI. Do not get drawn into chitchat and banter but keep focused on the purpose of your meeting with them.

What are the risks and what will be on offer?

One of the main risks is paying for the full course in advance of starting. This is often a requirement laid out in the contract. As always, before you sign anything, be aware of the small print. It may state that if, for some reason, you are unable to start the course or are unsuccessful in completing any part of the course, the fee or the remainder is not refundable. This will mean you lose all your money.

A better way to pay for your training is to pay for each part of the course individually and only pay for the next part when you have successfully completed the previous part of the course.

Also in the small print there may be a non-refundable proportion of the fee for administration. Check out how big this fee is and whether you consider it to be a fair payment.

There is always the risk of you not being successful in passing any of the three tests, and remember that the final instructional Part 3 test is by far the most difficult. You could get this far, having spent £2,000–£3,000, and still not pass. This is why you need to consider carefully whether this career is for you.

Questions you should ask

Before you sign anything, ask plenty of questions in order to find out whether your trainers are good at their job and whether you are going to receive good value for your money. Such questions might be as follows:

☐ How much does the course cost?

☐ Can I pay on a lesson-to-lesson basis or do I have to pay fees in advance?

☐ If so, how much? Do I have to pay for the whole course or can I pay for each part at a time, as I pass the exams?

☐ Can I get a refund if, for reasons beyond my control (e.g. contracting a serious illness or being unable to pass an exam), I cannot complete the course?

☐ Is there a non-refundable administration charge? If so, how much is it?

☐ Is all this written into the contract?

☐ May I take a copy of the contract away at the end of the meeting?

☐ Does the contract have a 'cooling-off period' written into it? Even if it does, get it home before you even think about signing it. Do not let them use this cooling-off period/clause as a way of getting you to sign on the spot. Inform them that you have other driving trainers to meet.

☐ Can I take the Part 1 on my own and then take Parts 2 and 3 with the training establishment? By how much will this reduce the overall cost?

☐ How long has the training establishment been in the business of training?

☐ How many successful trainees have they had? What is this as a percentage for each part of the course?

☐ What is each trainer's pass rate with their trainees on each of the three tests? Look at the figures carefully. A 100% pass rate, having taken just three trainees, will not tell you much.

☐ What grade is each of their trainers (see Appendix 2).

Also find out the following:

☐ If the school employs several trainers, can you choose your trainer? If possible, meet them all.

☐ Will I have the same trainer throughout?

☐ What is their training programme? How long will it take and what subjects does it cover? Can I take away a copy of the syllabus?

☐ What proportion of the course is spent in the classroom? For Parts 2 and 3, it should *not* be very long.

☐ For Parts 2 and 3, will the tuition be one-to-one, or will each trainer have two or three other trainees in the car? Is one-to-one training available and, if so, does it cost more? If there are several trainees in the car, the training establishment will make more money in less time. It can also be argued that having several trainees in the car can be helpful to the learning process and no doubt that point will be made if you ask. Nevertheless there are financial benefits to the training establishment. It is for you to decide whose best interest they have in mind.

☐ Whose car will you be using? If they suggest your car, would this be better for you? (It might be easier for you on the Parts 2 and 3 tests.) Negotiate a reduction in fees to take account of fuel bills and extra mileage on your car. If they do not agree to this then ask to use their car – they may not have one available, in which case they may have been economical with the truth. You can gain an insight from these little moments.

☐ If you do not have a car will they guarantee to loan one to you for your Parts 2 and 3 tests? Will this be written into the contract? Will this be at an additional cost to you?

☐ Can they guarantee the number of training hours per week that you want and at the times convenient to you? Will this be written into the contract?

☐ On your Part 3 course, will you have other trainees in the car during your 40 hours? In our opinion, this is not good practice.

Before you go for your interview

Before you go for your interview, print all these questions on to a sheet of paper. Have a heading entitled 'Training establishment' and fill in the establishment's name by hand. This will let them know they are not the only establishment you are looking at. Tick the questions off as you get the replies. That way you should not be diverted – intentionally or otherwise – from your task. If after you return home you find some questions have not been answered, contact them again. Obtain their answers in writing.

Do not commit yourself to a contract, yet

Once you have received all your answers, thank them, say goodbye and leave with a copy of the contract together with a copy of the training syllabus. Inform them that you need some cooling-off time to consider the offer and that you may contact them over the next few days to clarify any points or to accept a place on their course. Tell them that, before you make a final decision, you have appointments with other schools and you wish to hear what they are offering.

Any businessperson should admire your strategy. It is probably exactly how they would deal with it. If they try to pressure you into signing anything, tell them you do not want this pressure. If they persist and it makes you unhappy, walk away. Whatever you do, do not sign anything until you have had time to consider everything, coolly and calmly. Do not be swayed by a cheerful and friendly manner. These people may be driving instructors and projecting a friendly personality is part of what they do. They have had years of practice.

If you know anyone whose advice you would respect, ask them what they think of the training establishment's package. Look at the contract carefully. If you have any doubts or questions then contact them. If part of the contract states that you have to pay for the full course in advance, try to renegotiate paying for one part at a time. Now that you are out of their immediate grasp they may be more willing to give way on something like this. If they will not, read the warnings stated above and then think very carefully before you make your next move.

If you have any doubts and feel that, due to pressure, you may end up signing a contract before the meeting ends, leave your credit cards and cheque book at home.

Do you know that you may be entitled to a career loan? For more information, see Appendix 1.

3
Your training

❝ In Chapter 1 we outlined the structure of the Parts 1, 2 and 3 tests and looked at the training syllabus used by the Driving School Pro ADI Training School. In this chapter we take a closer look at the training process. ❞

ADI Part 1 training (theory)

When should you start preparing for this test?

Immediately! Send off to the DSA for the starter pack (ADI 14). Once received, complete the criminal records check form and send it to the appropriate address as soon as possible. With the starter pack you may also receive the ADI Part 1 *Theory Test Question Bank*, which contains all the questions for the Part 1 test. On the test you will be asked to answer 100 questions taken from this question bank. The withdrawl of this question bank is currently being considered.

Please do not learn these questions and answers 'parrot fashion.' If you are going to become an instructor you will need an in-depth knowledge of your trade. You will have questions, easy and difficult, fired at you by your clients. If they are to have any faith in you, you must know the answers.

Recommended books

In Table 1 we have set out a list of books that are judged to be essential background reading *before* you even think about going through the question bank. Once you consider that you have a good understanding of the subject, then use the question bank as a mock test. Answer, say, 50 at a time. If this 'mock test' highlights problems in specific areas, then concentrate on those questions. Do not be fooled if you did well in certain fields as a direct result of guesswork. You may not be so lucky on the day. Make sure you know your subject inside out.

Table 1 Essential background reading

Subjects	Books
Road procedures:	Highway Code; Driving: The Essential Skills
Traffic signs and signals	Highway Code; Know Your Traffic Signs
Car control	Driving: The Essential Skills
Pedestrians	Highway Code
Mechanical knowledge	The Motor Car: Mechanical Principles
Driving test	The Driving Instructor's Handbook; Instructional Techniques; ADI Starter Pack Practice for Driving Instructors; The Official Theory Test for Car Drivers; Hazard Perception (CD-ROM)
Disabilities	Driving: The Essential Skills; Instructional Techniques; The Driving Instructor's Handbook; ADI Starter Pack Practice for Driving Instructors
Law	Highway Code; Driving: The Essential Skills; The Official Theory Test for Car Drivers; Hazard Perception (CD-ROM)
Instructional techniques	The Driving Instructor's Handbook; Driving: The Essential Skills; publications from Driving School Pro

Note: Full details of the above publications can be found in Appendix 1.

Most candidates should be able to study for Part 1 on their own, but if you feel that you would benefit from professional advice, you might consider attending a short course designed to help you with this test. Please note that courses can be expensive, so be wary of Part 1 courses that last longer than one day. Remember, before you sign anything investigate carefully what you are committing yourself to (see Chapter 2 for more information). Ask the questions!

The Part 1 test

Once you have prepared yourself thoroughly by studying each topic at a time, say over a three to four week period, you should be ready to book your test (see Appendix 2). Part 1 tests are carried out at your local theory test centres – the same centres where learner drivers attend for their theory tests.

Currently, there is no limit to the number of attempts you can take but, obviously, each attempt will cost you more money, so it is good to go to the test confident and well prepared.

ADI Part 2 training (practical driving)

Choosing a trainer

You will be informed of your result at the end of the Part 1 theory test. If you have passed, you will be given a form which will enable you to apply for the Part 2 driving test. This is when you will need to obtain assistance from a professional instructor who undertakes ADI training. It would be beneficial if you know an ADI who can recommend a local trainer to you.

Another way would be to visit your local driving test centre, wait until all the candidates have left for the test, introduce yourself to the ADIs and ask if anyone can recommend a local trainer. If they do recommend one, you should gently probe as to why they think this trainer is good. If you do not feel you can do this, then use *Yellow Pages*, Google or any other suitable directory. Ring the local driving schools, explain what you want and see what they can advise.

Driving lessons

Once you have signed on with a trainer, they should take you out on driving lessons on a regular basis. You will no doubt be very surprised about the amount of driving faults that are pointed out to you. (Nearly everyone has a rather optimistic view of their driving abilities!) Do not be alarmed about this – it's just a matter of re-educating yourself and your driving reflexes. Take note of what your instructor tells you about where the problems lie and try to pre-empt them when you are driving.

In other words, think before you do it: do not keep making the same mistakes. The quicker you can get the problems sorted, the cheaper it should be for you. Make a list of your faults at the end of every session. Consult the list between lessons and before you go out on your own to practise.

Practise, practise, practise

Between training sessions, get out in your car and practise, practise, practise. Remember everything your instructor has spoken about (consult the list) and work on those problem areas. Remember, you must drive in a particular style and at an advanced standard. Consider joining the Royal Society for the Prevention of Accidents (RoSPA) or the Institute of Advanced Motorists (IAM). You will receive invaluable free training in advanced driving. You may even consider, if time allows, doing one of these courses before you even get anywhere near the Part 2 training stage.

Part 2 training is likely to take about 20–30 hours. You will need this time to shake the bad driving habits out of your system. (As mentioned before, you will most likely have far more than you realised.) You will also need time to understand and practise the driving style and skills required for this rigorous test. The Part 2 driving test requires that you demonstrate to the examiner a broad spectrum of skills, from carrying out very frequent mirror checks, to carrying out reverse manoeuvres accurately and *safely* – and the first time! It is important that your trainer gives you periodic mock tests to measure your progress and to prepare you for the big day.

The Part 2 test

The test is taken at certain test centres around the country. These are shown in the ADI 14 pack. The senior examiner (SE) conducts the test. The car you use must fit the DSA's criteria. (Look at the DSAs website for the latest information).

At the test centre you will be asked to show your driving licence. If you use the new–style licence you must take both parts – the plastic ID card and the paper licence – as both parts make up the complete driving licence.

You should take the Part 1 pass certificate and the letter inviting you to your Part 2 test. You will be asked to sign a declaration regarding the insurance for the vehicle and that you are living at the address shown on the licence. You will also be asked to sign a health declaration.

Driving licence

If you have an old-style licence you must take other means of identification. The only one allowed now is a current/valid passport. If you do not have one, then you should exchange your old licence for a new, photo-style licence in plenty of time. Forms are available from a main post office. Complete the form and send it off to the DVLA with the fee and two passport-style photographs of yourself. Please check that the old-style paper licence with a passport is still acceptable. It may change in the future.

Two examiners!

You may be asked if you will allow another supervising examiner to attend the test. They will sit quietly in the back and monitor the examiner undertaking the test. This is for quality-control purposes. (The other examiner is checking to see how their colleague is carrying out the tests, so do not be concerned that two examiners are present.) *Note:* The supervising examiner cannot over-ride the result of the test.

You may also ask the examiner if they would allow your trainer to accompany you, if this is your wish.

Time and marking

The Part 2 test lasts for about an hour. The candidate for the Part 2 driving test must make no more than six minor faults and must not make any serious faults. A minor fault could be not looking at your mirror at the appropriate moment but without causing any problems to other road users. A serious fault could be not checking your mirror and consequently causing another driver behind to slow down as you move off or stop. It is that strict.

Remember that you only have three chances to pass the ADI Part 2 test. The pressure is on if you do not pass first time. If you do not pass the second time, you only have one chance left, and so the pressure mounts. So, *practise* and aim to pass first time.

ADI Part 3 training (instructional ability)

It is absolutely essential that you receive professional guidance for the Part 3 test. This test is most likely to be a totally new experience and you will need to be guided by someone who knows what they are doing, what they are talking about and what will be expected from you on the day.

Training for the Part 3 test may take from 20 hours (for the very talented, who can absorb information quickly and confidently present lessons to the clients) to the more usual 40 hours or even longer. The Part 3 test is the most difficult and demanding part of the course. Again candidates can only have three attempts at this test. To have the best possible chance of passing the first time, they should be confident that they have had enough training before they apply.

Observing normal driving lessons

We believe that, during the Part 3 course, you should also be given the opportunity to observe the delivery of normal driving lessons by sitting in as your trainer instructs learner drivers. The ADI trainer should also deliver 'normal' lessons to you while you take the role of a learner driver client.

Training resources

Your training establishment should provide you with good-quality lesson notes and plans for you to use during the Part 3 course and, very importantly, for you to use during the Part 3 test. If these are not available from your trainer, Graphic Briefings can be purchased from Driving School Pro (see Appendix 2).

Mock tests

Your instructor should periodically evaluate your progress with mock tests, which cover each of the topics. This will give you an insight into what to expect and also some idea of the pressure exerted on you by the Part 3 test.

The Part 3 test

As described earlier, the Part 3 test of instructional ability lasts for one hour and is in two phases. You will be expected to instruct on one of the 12 exercises in each phase (see Appendix 2). The purpose of this test is for the examiner to assess your ability to instruct.

Getting into character

The examiner will take on the role of your client and can choose a character to suit the lesson. The senior examiner will inform you of the lesson subject at the start of each phase. They may choose to be a different character for the second phase. (One gets the impression that the senior examiners rather enjoy this thespian aspect of their job!)

You *must* make sure that you understand what the examiner is telling you. Try very hard to get into character yourself and to conjure up an image of the 'client' portrayed by the senior examiner. Keep focused on what you are trying to teach them. (To clarify the situation, the role played by the senior examiner will from now on be referred to as the SE client.)

Aims and objectives

You must aim to cover each aspect of the topic and make sure that the SE client understands what is being asked of them. Offer support as necessary and in accordance with the SE client's stated experience and abilities. You should be able to identify their mistakes and their causes and, with corrections, should help prevent them making the same mistakes again.

Q & A technique

By using a Q & A session at the start of the lesson, you should be able to learn from your SE client about their last lesson, how it went, the progress made and any problems arising. The SE client is not likely to offer you any assistance. The examiner will expect you to use the Q & A technique to find out all about the SE client before you allow them to drive off. This information, coupled with your assessment of their driving, will allow you to judge how the rest of the 'lesson' should proceed. Remember also that the SE client will make other mistakes, some quite subtle. You will be expected to identify, analyse and correct these problems.

Instructional qualities

The trainee must:

☐ pitch the lesson according to the SE client's needs, ability and experience;

☐ be able to put the information across effectively and according to the client's level of understanding;

☐ demonstrate good Q & A techniques so they understand the SE client's abilities and level of understanding. This Q & A session will help prevent errors from being made. It also helps the SE client to realise the purpose of the task and the way the task should be carried out;

☐ be encouraging and positive and provide necessary feedback to the SE client;

☐ plan the lesson regarding delivering the briefing and also allowing time for the SE client to practise and, hopefully, to succeed;

☐ control the lesson. For example, if the SE client is showing signs of being argumentative, then you must deal with this calmly and diplomatically but at the same time using the appropriate amounts of firmness and assertiveness so that the SE client carries out the task in *your* way;

☐ use the dual controls only when absolutely necessary to avoid any collision or dangerous situation from developing; and

☐ do not forget to give feedback on completion of the lesson, including areas that were carried out well and those that need further work. Do not just offer criticism; you need also to give praise and encouragement. Leave enough time at the end for the SE client to ask questions. Conclude each of the two sessions within the allowed time.

At the end of the Part 3 test, the examiner will come out of role, terminate the session and then return to the office to consider whether you have passed or not. The examiner will complete the marking sheet by grading both parts of the test. Once that has been done, you will be informed of the result and your grades and you will be given a brief explanation of any serious failings.

Part 3 test grades

The grades are within a scale of 1 to 6. Grade 1 is the lowest, with grades 1–3 being a fail. Grades 4–6 are a pass. Grade 6 is the highest grade attainable. Each phase of the Part 3 test is graded and you must receive a Grade 4 or above for each phase to pass. For example, a Grade 3 for the first phase and a Grade 5 for the second phase will unfortunately result in an overall fail.

When you pass

If you pass you will be given the written results sheet along with a form to apply for your ADI licence (for the licence fees, see the DSAs website).

Only when you have passed the Part 3 test are you legally entitled to undertake driving instruction for financial reward without having to be under the supervision of an ADI – once you have received your green licence to display on the windscreen.

DSA check tests

It is a condition of your licence that you undertake a periodic check test. You will be asked to attend your local test centre to show that you are still providing instruction to at least a minimum standard. Within the first three to six months after qualifying, you should receive a letter from the DSA requesting that you attend your first check test. This is classed as an 'educational' check test to find out how you are getting on. You have the choice of being observed by the senior examiner, of giving a lesson to one of your clients or of using the senior examiner as your client in role play.

The check test takes an hour. Unless your standard is high, you will not normally be graded at this time. This will occur at your second check test, which may be within the following one to two years.

4
Choosing your car

In this chapter we consider what you should be looking for when you choose your driving school car. This is obviously a major investment and a very important choice for you. Remember the saying: buy in haste – regret at leisure!

Should you buy an old or a new car?

You should weigh up whether your present car is suitable for the purpose of giving driving lessons or whether you will have to buy a new one. It is certainly not essential to have a new car. If you are satisfied that your present car is suitable and reliable and that it can have dual controls fitted (see below), then you would probably be better off using it. You want to keep expenditure down to a minimum until you are established. Consider keeping your car for about two years to save the further expense of buying another car and fitting dual controls.

Delivering instruction during your Part 3 course should give you a valuable insight into what is required from a driving school car, so we do not recommend buying one before then.

Buying a new car

If you choose to buy a new car we would suggest that you look around and make a note of the different makes and models of cars other driving instructors are using. You will notice that, usually, they are small hatchbacks. This is because there is little overhang under the rear window, thereby making it easier for clients to judge distances for parking. Also, being smaller usually makes them more manoeuvrable. Furthermore, there is a perception among learners that smaller cars are easier to drive, which may influence them in choosing a driving school with this type of car.

Do not rush into making a choice. Do your homework first. For unbiased information, read *Which?* magazine or subscribe to their website. If you do not subscribe to this magazine you may find that it is available in your local reference library. Alternatively, look at articles in driving association magazines which are available to their members. Log on to the *Driver Training Today* website (see Appendix 1) to see what other ADIs have to say about the cars they are using.

Think about which colour to choose, from a practical point of view. Some colours show up dirt easier than others and, even if you do clean it every morning, it may be looking as though you had not towards the end of the day. Metallic paints do cost more but they help your car to stand out from the rest.

Check the health and safety issues

Compare the NCAP (New Car Assessment Programme) safety rating of the cars you are thinking of buying. Also check to see how secure they are against theft. *Which?* magazine will help you with this.

Check its reliability

Using the magazines and websites mentioned above, check out the reliability of the cars you have short-listed. Generally speaking, the Japanese are considered to be the manufacturers who produce the most reliable cars. Some other manufacturers have a poor reliability record and, obviously, these should be avoided.

Check whether your car can be used for the test

You should bear in mind that not all cars are allowed to be used for the driving test (e.g. the Vauxhall Tigre, the two-door 'Smart' car and the BMW Mini convertible). Two-seater cars are not allowed for the test. Check with the DSA if you intend to purchase a car that you have not seen used by other ADIs.

Some cars have been the subject of a manufacturer's recall to fix problems. On a very few occasions this has meant that the car has been temporarily banned from tests until the problem has been fixed, and proof of this is required. Look at the DSA website to see if the car you are intending to buy is mentioned. If it is, check that the work has taken place before you buy it. Verify that, if it has any unusual and exotic controls, they are acceptable for the test.

Buying dual controls

Make sure that dual controls are available for the model of car (especially if it is a new model). If you prefer one type of control (e.g. rod rather than cable), you should check to see if they can be fitted to that model.

Several firms in the UK produce dual controls. He-Man is probably considered to be the market leader. We have used He-Man and have had no problems with them. If you buy them new you can arrange to have them fitted at your home address or at the dealer's garage and, by agreement, by one of the regional He-Man-approved fitters. Having them fitted will cost extra and it is quite expensive. It is possible to fit them yourself if you feel confident to do so. Some local garages will fit them, but you will need to be confident in their abilities.

You may be able to purchase second-hand dual controls from adverts in various driving school magazines and via the Internet. Whichever dual control system you choose, check periodically that they are all freely moving for they may require lubrication or adjustment. Please note that some cars, due to their internal layout, cannot be fitted with rod-type controls.

Check which type of dual controls are available

Many ADIs prefer rod dual controls rather than cable ones. With the rod type you can have them set up to move or not to move the passenger-side pedals as the client depresses and realeases their pedals. With cable pedals operated by the driver, the dual controls remain static until operated by the ADI. We prefer the pedals to work in tandem because, when taking lessons with a novice in the dark, the ADI can feel the client's pedals move by gently resting a foot on top of the appropriate pedal.

Replacing the dual controls or the car?

As dual controls are expensive, when your car comes to the end of its working life you might consider replacing it with the same model. This way you can swap the dual controls over. So, be sure that the car you initially purchase is one that you really like by undertaking a thorough selection process and test drive.

If you are going to use a six-month trainee licence our advice is either to buy some second-hand dual controls for your present personal car (check they are available) or to hire a dual-controlled car for the six months. This way, if things do not work out, your outlay will be kept to a minimum. For contact details of the two major suppliers of dual controls, see Appendix 1.

Choosing a petrol or a diesel engine car

Consider the advantages of diesel for driving lessons. Diesel cars have less of a tendency to stall, which will give clients confidence during the early lessons. If you do have a diesel-powered car, however, it is tempting to let clients rely over-much on the low-rev torque (for example, when pulling away without using the accelerator). You should bear in mind that, once they have passed the test, they may be driving a petrol car. Do ensure that your clients therefore drive the diesel as though it were a petrol-driven car. Remember also that some motorists believe that cheap supermarket diesel fuel may lead to fuel injector problems.

This is a complicated choice, so you should consider:

- the initial vehicle cost;

- the cost of diesel and petrol (often increases after each budget);

- the amount of miles covered per annum;

- depreciation;

- service costs and road tax (again, often increase after each budget).

The arguments for and against petrol and diesel engines

Consider our arguments for and against, as shown below, and perhaps use Internet sites to give you further up-to-date guidance:

- Diesel cars are more expensive to buy but usually hold their resale value better.

- There is usually a better mpg from a diesel, but the gap is closing as advances are made in petrol engine technology.

- Diesel fuel is currently more expensive to buy in the UK.

- Diesel cars may not be as eco-friendly – but there are arguments on both sides. Diesel cars emit less CO_2 as they are more efficient than petrol cars, but they produce more nitrogen oxide and particulate matter.

- Diesel cars are less likely to stall than a petrol car, which is a bonus when teaching learners to drive.

- Petrol cars take around a mile to warm up. Once the engine is up to full operating temperature, though, a petrol engine is usually cleaner than that of a diesel and it gives out lower emissions.

- Diesel engine technology has advanced rapidly over the last few years. Their reputation of being noisy, smelly, slow to start or slow to accelerate is mostly a thing of the past, and they can be very pleasant to drive.

- Usually, both types have similar service intervals but diesels may require more oil changes.

☐ It is considered by experts that if you return a high (over 20,000) annual mileage, diesel is the better option (20,000–30,000 miles per annum is certainly not unusual for a driving school car).

Considering the costs

Hiring or leasing versus buying a car

You can choose to buy or hire your car (for more information, see later in this chapter). Whichever method you choose to use, you should obviously shop around for the best deal. Contact the garages, explain that you are a driving instructor and see what they are prepared to offer. Apart from any local offer, some manufacturers have national promotions for driving schools which may include a reduced price, free dual controls, free signs, etc. Check out their websites. Go to garages with Internet prices to hand and haggle.

Towards the end of the month and quarter are the best times to seek a new(er) car to buy. If the sales during the month or quarter are low, the salesperson is more likely to agree a far lower price. Remember that, when you buy a new car, you are paying VAT. Why give the government tax on the purchase of a new car? Seek one that is either a year old or pre-registered (a demonstrator).

Compare the costs of diesel and petrol vehicles. Check out the service intervals and costs. Find out if there are any particularly expensive service items, such as renewing the cam belt (timing chains last longer). Check what level of warranty is provided with the car and over what time/miles. Look at the manufacturer's figures for fuel consumption. These can be on the optimistic side, so check on the Internet to find any independent figures.

What do you really need in your car?

When you are ordering your new car, consider carefully what you actually need in and on it. Do not get carried away when the salesperson brings out their catalogue of extra goodies. It is very easy when you are spending thousands of pounds on a new car to start believing a few hundred extra here or there is not going to matter. Think how many lessons it would take to cover these items. For example, do you really need a fitted satellite navigation system that you will lose when you sell the car? It makes more sense to buy a portable model that can be transferred from car to car. Do you need those very expensive bits of plastic kit stuck on to the outside? Yes, they look very nice, but who apart from you is going to be that impressed?

No matter how careful you are and no matter how quick you are, the chances are that your car will be kerbed more than once during its working life. This is bad enough if it just damages the new wheel trims but, if it damages the alloys, then that could be an expensive bill. So alloys are probably better avoided.

Considering the depreciation values of cars

Look at the depreciation values. Some cars depreciate quicker than others. This is a major factor when the time comes to up-grade your car.

Do not forget the additional costs, such as roof signs, magnetic signs and the dual controls.

Choosing a convenient garage

When choosing a convenient garage, ask yourself the following questions:

☐ Are you going to use a franchised garage to do the servicing? If so, is there one near to you?

☐ When you put your car in for a service, will the garage come and collect it and return it after the service?

☐ If, due to your work patterns, you can only have the car serviced at weekends, is the garage going to be open?

☐ Does the car have to be serviced at a franchise garage? If not, you can use your local, reputable garage, which may save you a great deal of money over time. Check, however, that this will not affect your warranty.

Buying your car

Once you have completed your research, make a list of suitable cars and then make an appointment with the dealers to have a test drive.

When buying a new car, what will your salesperson offer you? You may have a bit of purchasing muscle here. Your car will be an excellent advert for the particular make. Not only will it be seen being used by a driving school (which should indicate that it is reliable and easy to drive) but clients are also inclined to buy the same model of car in which they learnt to drive. You may even consider making a commission arrangement for each client or instructor who buys a car from the franchise garage on your recommendation – say, £75 per car.

Before and during the test drive let the salesperson be aware that you are shopping around for a driving school car and that you want the best deal you can get.

When buying a new car, you should make sure you choose one that is going to fit all your needs. Below we describe some of the features you should consider. In Appendix 5 you will find a checklist of items that you should be looking for when buying a new car and of what you should be looking for when you take any car out for a test drive.

It is doubtful that there is such a thing as a perfect car but, by using the information below, you should be able to get fairly close to this ideal.

Is it a comfortable car?

The car should be comfortable, be a pleasure to drive and a pleasure to be a passenger in. There should be no annoying squeaks and rattles and the doors should close with a solid, well built clunk.

The car will be your office and you will have to sit in it for most of you working day. The seats should not be too soft and they should offer good support for your back. Make sure that the seats can be adjusted over a reasonably wide range – both up and down and backwards and forwards – to accommodate clients of all builds.

The seats should be sturdy and well constructed as some of your clients may be on the very large side. Some cheaper cars have flimsy seats that will probably not stand the test of time. Seat covering material should be able to breath – it should not be shiny or slippery and it should not be difficult to keep clean. The driver should be able to sit tall in the seat, which will give them a view of the kerb close to the car.

Do you need air conditioning?

Air conditioning is strongly recommended. This will allow you to drive with the windows up, shutting out a lot of the traffic noise, fumes and dust while keeping the temperature at a comfortable level. Air conditioning will also help prevent the seats becoming affected by sweat during the hot months.

In the winter, using the air conditioning in conjunction with hot air will quickly demist your car's windows and keep them clear throughout the day. You will find this especially important on cold, wet days when misting windows can become a real problem. This is very noticeable if you have to leave the windows closed with the engine switched off during longish lesson briefings. Air conditioning will rapidly clear the windows before you set off again.

Choosing the engine

If the car is fitted with a turbocharger, make sure that the effects of any increased speed as it starts to operate will not be too much for a learner to handle. The engine management system should not cause too much of a compensating surge of speed when the revs drop while the car is in the lower gears – for example, when the car is going around sharp junctions with no gas and in second gear.

Look carefully at the foot and hand controls

The foot controls

The foot pedals should be comfortable to use, not offset, not too high (for those with small feet) and/or not too close together. The clutch should be smooth and the bite point should be comfortable, predictable and progressive. The footbrake should be progressive and smooth. The car should take up the drive in first gear smoothly and without snatching. The gas pedal should also be smooth in operation and should control the speed in a calm and manageable way.

The car's hand controls

The steering wheel should be adjustable. The steering should be power assisted and a small turning circle will be helpful on the manoeuvres. The gears should be easy to select without baulking or feeling notchy. Reverse gear should be easy to achieve. Ideally, it should not be close to fourth or fifth gear as clients do sometimes mistake the change. To push the gear stick down or to lift the collar to select reverse is far better.

The handbrake lever should feel sturdy rather than flimsy. Indicators, light switches, etc., should be logical, should feel robust and should fall easy to hand. We advise strongly against buying a car with indicators on the right-hand side of the steering wheel. Most older, Japanese cars (for example) are like this. Your clients will be extremely confused if the cars they are practising in at home have the indicators on the left-hand side of the steering wheel, which is now common.

The driver's view through the windows

The views through all windows, not forgetting the rear and rear-side windows, should be good. There is a tendency at the moment for manufacturers to fit smaller windows. The door mirrors should be large and electrically adjustable.

During the test drive, see if you can keep the kerb in view in the corner of the rear window when reversing around a sweeping/long corner. If this cannot be seen, consider using aids such as wide-angle mirrors fitted to the door mirror and/or booster cushions (see Chapter 11).

What instrumentation do you want?

Instruments, especially the speedometer, should be easy to see and to read. On some cars the speedometer cannot be seen from the passenger seat. This may mean that you will need to buy an auxiliary instrument that can be fitted where you can see it. Check the manufacturer can provide one or see Appendix 1 for an alternative supplier. Digital displays are usually larger and clearer than analogue instruments.

The DSA are now insisting that auxiliary speedometers are positioned in a safe position (e.g. not on the dashboard where they could interfere with the deployment of the airbag in the event of an accident). They must also be fitted by the car manufacturer's franchise garage.

Does your car have good lighting?

Interior lighting should be good as you will no doubt be doing briefings in the dark. Exterior bulbs should be easy to change but, with newer models, this is becoming awkward and time consuming. Modern car design has made the changing of some exterior bulbs take on almost epic proportions. Some cars may even need to have the bumper removed to gain access.

If the examiner finds your vehicle has a defective light, they will cancel the test. This will result in one very disappointed client and, unfairly, a slight knock to your reputation. If you do have a test cancelled for this reason and you run a reputable driving school, you will also feel obliged to refund the test fee to your client and to give a couple of hours free tuition before the next test. Do not think that this is an unlikely event. You just have to raise the subject with other ADIs in a driving test waiting-room to hear of their bad experiences.

Is there adequate space?

The distance between driver and passenger should be comfortable. There should be ample storage space for all your files, books, pens and records. The boot space should be adequate for your needs. If you think that reaching for your books and folders off the back seat is going to be a problem or that you will be carrying rear-seat passengers on a regular basis, then perhaps you should consider a five-door car rather than a three door.

What type of spare wheel does it have?

Check what form of spare wheel is carried. Quite often the spare wheel that is provided is a space saver – a small and thin temporary wheel, designed to get you to the nearest garage. The DSA will not allow these to be fitted to an axle for the test. The only way around this problem is to buy a car with a full-sized spare wheel or replace the space saver in the boot with a standard wheel, should it be necessary to change a punctured tyre before the start of the test. As space-saver wheels are becoming more and more common, you may have to accept the risk.

Taking a test drive

When you take a car out for a test drive you should not be fobbed off with a spin around the block. Give it a good workout. Try to take the car out on your own. Some dealers will offer 24–72 hour test drives. If this is not possible and you find that the salesperson cannot keep quiet during the drive, ask them (politely) to let you evaluate the car without being distracted.

You should get into learner driver territory on the housing estates, etc. Put the car through a simulated lesson. Drive it around sharp junctions and go through the reversing exercises. Check out everything you would be expecting your client to cope with. If you have a salesperson with you, ask them to drive for a short period so you can look at the situation from the instructor's seat. Use the checklist (see Appendix 5) to make sure the car will fit the bill.

Buying, leasing or hiring a car?

This choice will be influenced by whether you want to own your car outright or whether you are happy to lease it off a company – in effect renting the vehicle. If you wish to buy the car you will need to choose whether you want to pay in one cash payment, arrange a loan or pay by instalments to a finance company.

You may be offered an instalment plan at the garage but, as this is quite a competitive market, before signing any agreement, shop around for the best deal. Some credit card companies have 0% offers for six to nine months. If you could pay this back within the time, it's a cheap loan. In order to appreciate how much the deal is going to cost, look at the annual percentage rate (APR) and the total amount repayable. *Do not* be misled by the flat rate which is often quoted by dealers. Dealers may be prepared to haggle over the APR.

Remember that, when you use hire purchase, you will not own the car until the final payment has been made, so you will not be able to sell it without the agreement of the finance company. On the other hand, if you do buy under a hire-purchase scheme and anything goes wrong with the car, the lender is jointly responsible with the dealer for fixing it.

Further important considerations

If you buy, you will be able to:

- [ ] use the car over an unlimited number of miles;

- [ ] have the choice as to whether you change your cars more frequently; and

- [ ] obtain cheaper insurance because your choice will not be limited by a contract with a hire firm.

You must also consider:

- [ ] the car's depreciation over the time you expect to keep it;

- [ ] the problems of selling a car with high mileage;

- [ ] the cost of purchasing and fitting dual controls;

- [ ] the cost of servicing the car; and

- [ ] the problems of having no substitute vehicle if it breaks down.

If you hire you may:

- [ ] have to pay an additional fee if you exceed the contract's mileage limit;

- [ ] have to keep the car for the extent of the contract period;

- [ ] have the servicing, road fund licence, tyres, insurance, breakdown cover and mechanical repairs included in the contract fee; and

- [ ] receive a replacement car with 24 hours in the event of a no-fault accident or long-term mechanical problem.

But do:

☐ read the contract's terms and conditions carefully; and

☐ consider the implications of loss of income you are if incapacitated through illness or injury or if you are financing your car by regular repayments. Consider taking out an insurance policy to cover such an eventuality.

Buying a new car is a massive investment for most people, and we suggest you consider all the options very carefully. We do not have the space in this book to give you more than a brief outline of financing the purchase of a car. If you subscribe to the *Which?* website you will find totally unbiased, up-to-date and very useful information on cars and how to buy them. *Which?* reports are unbiased because they do not take any adverts or become involved commercially in any way with manufacturers or other commercial organisations. They are 100% for the consumer, which is unique.

5
The ADI as a businessperson

This chapter explains the implications of running your own business.

Running a successful business

Your business should do well if you:

☐ have a good, friendly, professional approach to all your clients;

☐ have a high pass rate;

☐ get clients through their driving test with few driving faults and in the shortest time possible;

☐ obtain most of your clients from recommendations;

☐ keep a full diary;

☐ keep good accounts of your financial activities;

☐ keep yourself and your car clean and tidy;

☐ are punctual for lessons;

☐ use good and effective training aids and keep good records of your clients' progress;

☐ keep up to date with DSA news;

☐ know who is going to answer the telephone; and

☐ have the means to answer client's calls or to reply to messages quickly.

Setting up a home office

Ideally, every ADI should have a room/office that is devoted to their driving business. If possible it should be well away from disturbances.

The office environment

We are not going to list everything that your office should contain, but you will find below items we consider essential:

☐ Buy a good, fast printer for your PC, especially if you are printing your own brochures, logbooks, etc. Quite often manufacturers will almost give their printers away. The reason is that, once you have bought them, you will then have to buy the ink cartridges or toners from the manufacturer. Compare the prices of these items before you decide. Also consider buying recycled ink cartridges or toners but be warned that using them may negate your warranty.

☐ Keep your PC in good working order by using anti-virus software, anti-spyware software and a firewall. Keep your hard disk defragged and use the Windows tools to keep everything running smoothly. Back up important files on a regular basis. (For free, good-quality anti-virus software and free anti-spyware software to download from the net, see Appendix 1).

☐ Make sure you have a lot of storage and worktop space.

☐ Have at least one filing cabinet to file documents in alphabetical order.

☐ Keep an old PC as a standby.

☐ Back up storage for your PC files. It is vital that you save your data regularly on to storage media other than your PC's hard drive. Use a second disk drive, CD, DVD or storage key. An external hard drive plugged into a USB port is quite cheap, quick and very simple to use. (The hard drive used in our office is Western Digital My Book 250GB and the piece of mind it brings is well worth the price.) Some experts recommend that, when not in use, any external hard drives should be unplugged to avoid virus attack. To make this task easier, consider investing in a powered USB hub with extension lead so the hard drive can be easily unplugged on the desktop.

☐ Keep a good stock of office supplies.

☐ Have good lighting.

☐ Ideally, you will have someone at home to answer the telephone – but this may not always be possible. There are two alternatives. One is to have an answer phone, and the other is to have it routed to your mobile via a BT service. The problem with the answer phone is that you will not be able to speak directly with your caller. This may lead to lost opportunities. Any answer phone greeting message should be friendly, informative and as short as possible. If you have a website, ask them to access this in the message. Ask callers to leave their telephone number for you to return their call by the end of the day. The problem with having the call routed to your mobile is twofold. A client may resent the fact that you are dealing with business matters during *their* paid lesson. Secondly, there will be a conflict between listening to the caller on your hands-free mobile while driving and giving a lesson. Remember that it is illegal for an ADI supervising a lesson in progress to use a handheld telephone.

☐ Have a telephone number display box linked to your office/landline phone. This is plugged into your phone line and sits on your desk. Before the telephone is answered you can see the number of the caller, unless it is withheld. This displays incoming numbers with the time and date of the call, keeping these until deleted, until full (approximately 100 calls) or until the battery is exhausted.

☐ You could consider having a dedicated line solely for your business – both landline and mobile. If you do, you will know that, when a certain phone rings, you will answer it in the appropriate manner. Initial greetings are important.

And remember to keep your office tidy!

If you are going to purchase any peripherals (e.g. printers or hard drives), we suggest that you log on to Amazon.com. Use the customers' reviews to find out what they thought of the items they have bought.

Your Income

What level of income can you realistically expect to earn?

Income for many self-employed professionals can be unpredictable. Being an ADI is no exception. Advertising selectively to save outgoing costs and receiving much of your work through recommendations, particularly by getting your clients through their test in good time and first time, could see you with a full diary – given time. Remember not to pitch your fees too low. It is then a question of maintaining a high pass rate and, by giving your clients 5–10 business cards to spread around on their first and last lesson, they will do your advertising for you.

A 30-hour week should return a minimum £600 gross. Remember also to encourage two-hour lessons to reduce 'dead time' travelling to and from lessons. This is explored further a little later in this chapter.

Lesson fees

Lesson fees vary widely across the country, so we cannot be specific on what you should charge. Our best advice is to investigate the range of lesson prices in your area and to pitch your fees initially in the middle of these until you become known and your good reputation spreads. You can then gradually increase your lesson fees.

If you adopt a cut-throat approach to lesson fees and undercut your opposition, you should be aware that other ADIs might not be too friendly towards you. Undercutting their fees considerably will not encourage them to welcome you into their area or into their local association. Remember, you will be talking to them each time you meet at the test centres. Instructors do talk to each other and always about the new ADIs in their area. On the other hand, if times are desperate and you feel that this is the only way to get your toe in the door, then you may have to do it.

Dealing with clients

Cancellations

You should anticipate that lesson cancellations can happen on a weekly basis. Unless you take on more clients than you require you will earn less than you predicted. Allow for this when taking on clients or when you set the parameters of your working day/week. To cover this problem, some ADIs take on about two or three more clients than they need. If you show your clients (when arranging the next lesson) that you have a very busy diary, perhaps with lessons being booked three weeks ahead, they will be very reluctant to cancel a lesson. In the early days you can pad out your diary with 'ghost' clients, but make sure you remember who they are so you can erase them later on – you do not want the taxman to benefit at your expense.

Losing clients

You should realise that you will inevitably lose the occasional client to another driving school. The most common reasons are that the client can obtain cheaper lessons elsewhere, they think they are at test standard despite your advice or the chemistry between you isn't right. You will both recognise this last problem and it should be acceptable, but rare. Do not worry about it too much because you will most likely receive clients from your competitors for the same reason.

How are clients and instructors chosen?

Although by no means foolproof, we believe you can choose your clients to some degree by the price of your lessons. If you pitch your lesson fees low, do not be surprised if many of those who contact you are unemployed, employed part time or are on a low income. As a result you will receive more appointment cancellations.

Callers will often base their choice on the instructor's sales pitch. This will then lead to callers either booking a lesson there and then or stating they will ring you back – but they may not. Your 'sales pitch' should not be, or sound, over-bearing. Be friendly and listen to their questions, then answer them with points you wish to state. Your potential client will be assessing you over the course of the call, so the way you answer the telephone, what you say and how you say it are all important.

Managing your time

Working unsociable hours

You will probably work beyond the 9–5 norm, particularly in the early stages of your career. It is essential that you put yourself in the position of your potential clients. Those who are employed or at home looking after the house and children may not be able to have driving lessons until the evening or at weekends.

Client time-restraints

Some clients may only have the same period free during the week and every week. College students may be a bit more flexible, depending on their term timetable. The unemployed are usually flexible, unless they have family commitments. Remember that you cannot accommodate them all at the same time. It is very important that, when an inquirer calls, you ask them at what time and day they could have their lessons and make sure that space is usually available in your diary.

Consider the clients you want. Do you want clients who are available during the daytime (e.g. students, the unemployed, housewives/househusbands, those who need babysitters) or are these the ones who will be very money conscious and more likely to cancel lessons? Are you looking for clients who believe that, by paying more, they will be receiving a better-quality instructor and that the lesson fee is of lesser importance? Clients in this bracket are usually the more reliable but may require lessons outside normal working hours. In reality, you will have a cross-section of the population. But, if you charge more than the average for your area, you are likely to have more employed clients who may also be older and who are less likely to cancel lessons due to financial constraints.

Time flexibility

You will need to be flexible with your working hours. Some instructors enjoy a mid-week day off as it breaks up the intensity of the hours and days worked. Some ADIs will work all the hours they can get.

A good compromise is to work one or two late evenings – perhaps starting late on these days and one weekend day to accommodate those who cannot make a weekday. Many instructors do not work weekends, and this could be a niche market you might consider exploiting.

Leisure time

Remember, you have or should have an outside life. Sitting in a car for hours on end is not good for you – we know that from experience. Even if you are not a particularly active person, it is important to take some exercise and have other interests or you will soon 'go stale'. Enjoy giving driving tuition but enjoy other aspects of life as well, especially your family.

So consider the following:

☐ How many days do you wish to work?

☐ Are you going to set aside half a day to undertake 'office work'?

☐ What days do you wish to work?

☐ How early will you start? The first driving test of the day is at 08:40. With the hour lesson in front, plus travelling time, this may mean you having to leave the house at 07:15, or earlier!

☐ How late in the day will you work? Consult your partner. What time do you want to eat?

☐ How many weeks (unpaid) holiday will you take?

☐ How far from home are you willing to work? Travelling time does not create income – it creates cost. Think of fuel, car-servicing schedules, car components (tyres, brake pads, etc.) and additional car depreciation due to high mileage.

Build in time to take on board fuel for your car and yourself, for toilet stops, thinking/unwinding time, traffic delays, up-dating records, making telephone calls, updating business accounts, banking, cleaning the car, etc.

Time off work

If you are self-employed you will not be paid for any time you take off. This includes holidays and sickness. Sickness or injury can strike anyone at any time and, unfortunately in this job, there is no such thing as a paid 'sicky'. No work = no income. Take care of your health and think carefully before you book that skiing holiday. Later in this chapter you will find reference to accident, injury and sickness insurance you may wish to consider.

When you need a break, consider the time of the year or days/weekends (such as bank holidays) when there may be an increase in holiday traffic in your area. To work over such a period may also result in cancelled lessons due to clients being away.

Income

How much do you want to earn and when?

Considering some of the above points, you can work out approximately how much you will earn each week/month/year.

Example

Let us say that you wish to earn £600 per week gross for 48 weeks a year – which takes into account days off over Christmas, Easter, bank holidays (when it may be chaotic on the roads), annual leave holidays and periods of sickness. Your estimated annual gross income is therefore £28,800.

You wish to work five days a week, say at about £120 per day. The lesson prices must therefore be £20 per hour:

$$£20 \times 30 \text{ hrs a week} \times 48 \text{ wk} = £28,800 \text{ per year gross}$$

If you want to earn more, consider increasing your lesson fee rate a little and work, say, an extra half day a week or an hour longer each day. Remember, though, that if you intend raising your lesson fees, do it when you are busy. You could realistically earn £36,960 per year gross (£22 x 35 x 48).

Suppose most of your lessons are two hours in duration and you receive a cancellation that you cannot fill with another client. We therefore suggest you consider booking seven hours a day. If you have a rare full week you could earn around £700 – depending on your geographical location.

You might consider charging more for a single hour to encourage two hour lessons and less wasted time to and from clients.

Perhaps your 30-hour working week (allowing for meal breaks) might be as follows:

Monday – day off		
Tuesday – afternoons/evenings 2–8p.m.	=	approx. 5 hours
Wednesday – all day 8.30 a.m.–5.30 p.m.	=	7
Thursday – a late day 10 a.m.–7.30 p.m.	=	8
Friday – standard day 9 a.m.–5 p.m.	=	6
Saturday – day off		
Sunday – short day 10 a.m.–4 p.m.	=	4
Total:		**30 hrs**

Thirty hours sounds like a nice short week, but this is your 'earning' time. When you factor in travelling times and office work, then you will see that the working week may well exceed 40 hours.

Income variations and holidays

Unfortunately there is no way you can guarantee a regular income throughout the year. Once well established, your income will become a great deal more predictable but, to start with, lessons will occur erratically throughout the week. You should also realise that there are seasonal changes.

During the period from the school Easter holiday through to around October, there is usually an enormous number of people wanting driving lessons. To cover the leaner winter months, you should aim to obtain new clients from September and October onwards. Many people do not like the idea of learning to drive in poor weather conditions or when it is dark. You may therefore need to consider revising your weekly working schedule to accommodate clients' wishes.

Approaching and throughout the Christmas period, those on a low income may vary their lesson appointments, the length of lessons or cancel lessons altogether. Those with birthdays and those receiving cash for Christmas presents (or driving lesson vouchers) may well want to start lessons from 26 December. Otherwise, inquiries may be in short supply until around March.

Your clients may want to use bank holidays for lessons but, if you live in a busy holiday/tourist area, you might consider watching the sport on television instead. Inform your clients that they may be paying good money just to sit in a traffic jam. You will also have the very real problem of trying to get to lesson appointments through the heavy traffic. Mondays are therefore a very good day to have as your rest day.

If you are looking to have an annual holiday during the summer time, this is one of your busier periods, so having a holiday at this time is not ideal. It is worth considering a winter holiday in a warmer climate.

With all the above in mind, you should now realise that you are not going to have a regular income throughout the year. Consider budgeting for this by having more lessons per week than you think you need, especially in the summer months.

Other forms of income

Finally, you may consider finding a source where you can purchase, at a discounted price, books and CD-ROMs related to the theory and practical driving tests. These you could sell on to clients at the usual retail price, making a small profit. You could also hire these out for a set time. (Remember, however, that the theory test question bank is altered every year, round about autumn, so do not get stuck with out-of-date stock.) You could also insist that, as part of their course, your clients buy a logbook in order to keep a record of their progress. These can be bought from Driving School Pro and sold at a profit (for sources of discs, books and logbooks, see Appendices 1 and 2).

Expenditure

When constructing your business plan, you will have to take *all* your costs into account. Because of price fluctuation and other variables, it is impossible to give figures in this book, but you should be able to obtain some idea of costs by checking prices on the Internet and asking questions on the ADI forums.

When considering your expenditure you should take account of the following:

☐ What type of car – manual or automatic (or are you going to run both?).

☐ Car servicing, depreciation, repairs, tyres, car cleaning and fuel.

☐ Roof and other signs.

☐ Subscriptions to professional organisations.

☐ The ADI licence every four years (see the DSA's website for current costs).

☐ Obtaining a good, cheap accountant. Talk to several before making a decision.

☐ Legal fees if you intend to draw up client–instructor contracts etc.

☐ County Court fees if you claim against clients for unpaid or cancelled lessons that are in breach of your terms and conditions.

☐ Stationery and computers and their repair/replacement.

☐ Telephone costs: landline and mobile.

☐ Bank charges (these sometimes start from the second year onwards). At the time of going to press, if you subscribe to the Federation of Small Businesses (FSB) and bank with the Co-operative Bank, you will not pay bank charges if your business account remains in credit. This is worth considering. Check first to confirm.

☐ Standing order's/direct debit's that transfer a set amount each month to your savings/retirement fund/pension account/health insurance account.

☐ Putting something away each week for your replacement car – this is cheaper than paying interest on a loan when the time comes to change it.

☐ Insurance to cover your accountant's bills if the Inland Revenue decides to check your accounts. This can be a very costly event. At the time of writing, this item should be covered if you subscribe to the FSB. Check first.

☐ Health insurance.

☐ A private pension.

☐ Advertising.

☐ Income tax.

☐ National Insurance contributions.

Advertising

In order to earn a good living, you should not need to have large, costly adverts in local newspapers and telephone directories. These are expensive and will make a large dent in your profits.

Standing out from the rest

Try to find a 'unique selling point': this is something that only your driving school will be offering locally. It could be that you specialise in teaching especially nervous customers. You may state that you are more than happy to take on middle-aged customers. Perhaps you could have an on-board video camera to record and playback the lessons, if the client wishes. One free hour of Pass Plus could be offered to everyone who passes the test with you. Free logbooks could be offered to all customers.

You may use Graphic Briefings to get your points across clearly and quickly (see Appendix 2). Give these matters some serious thought and give your imagination full rein. Do not be a follower of fashion, be a leader.

Where to advertise

We believe that you need to be seen out and about all the time with a roof sign showing your driving school name and contact details. We recommend that you have brochures and business cards to hand out to on-the-spot inquirers.

The brochure can take many forms. A newsletter format works well. You can include general information about the driving tests, useful websites and information about your prices, about who you are, your code of practice and terms and conditions. Give the newsletter a number (e.g. Newsletter No.133). This will give the impression of an established school. Desktop publishing software (DTP) is ideal for this. We recommend Serif Page Plus. Although this is not expensive considering what you get, you may be able to find even cheaper (older) versions on Ebay. You could respond to telephone inquirers by sending this brochure through the first-class post or by dropping it through their letterbox the same day.

Posters, business cards and flyers

You can easily produce advertising stationery on your computer. Your business card should show on one side:

☐ your driving school logo;

☐ your photo (head/shoulders – e.g. the same one as on your ADI licence);

☐ your telephone number;

☐ your website and email addresses; and

☐ logos of related associations/qualifications (e.g. DIA (Driving Instructor Association) or IAM Institute of Advanced Motorists)).

On the reverse side of your card you could include any of the following:

☐ your average driving test pass rate;

☐ any unique selling points;

☐ the terms and conditions for cancellation of lessons;

☐ that full details of your terms and conditions are shown on your website, or are provided at the first lesson or in advance of this by request;

☐ vehicle(s) used;

☐ areas covered;

☐ availability of lessons (days and times);

☐ your courses, with a brief description (e.g. ADI training: Parts 1, 2 and 3 to become a driving instructor).

We recommend that you have a good supply of business cards in the car and in your wallet or purse. Not only will people knock on your window but they will also stop you in filling stations to ask for details. Give each of your clients five at the end of their first lesson and when they pass their test to give to friends and family members who are, or may soon be, looking for a driving instructor. This type of recommendation is the best form of advertising.

Think about advertising on school and college noticeboards. Don't forget to ask for permission.

If times are hard, consider a lesson fee reduction to clients, for every new client they bring to your driving school.

Local newspapers

At the start you may need to place adverts in your local newspaper. Keep them brief. If you do use the newspapers make sure your advert appears where you want it and not in some throw-away motoring supplement.

Choose the right day. Think about when your potential customers and their parents are most likely to be looking for a driving instructor. Fridays and Saturdays are probably the best, when they are away from work/school and have the time to discuss driving lessons and read adverts.

When you place your advert, ask if there is a three for two price offer. If you do not want your competitors to know why you are advertising, be astute. (e.g 'Due to recent test passes a driving instructor now has vacancies …').

Internet website

Use the Internet to show the world your business details, your CV (if helpful), your lesson fees, terms and conditions, courses, general information, etc. A web presence in this day and age is very important, if not vital. More and more people are Googling when they are shopping around. We now receive more inquires from Googlers than *Yellow Pages*. If you do not have a website customers may draw their own negative conclusions.

Designing your own website

You can produce your own website using software such as Microsoft FrontPage. These programs may take a little bit of time to understand but it will be time well spent. It is usually just a process of trial and error.

If you can learn how to design and manage your own website this will save you a great deal of money, now and in the future. You will be able to access your website and update it whenever you want, rather than having to employ an IT 'expert'.

Once you start working on your new website you may find that it can be very interesting and absorbing. To obtain some ideas, look around at other websites. Do not get carried away with lots of coloured pages, busy fonts and too many pictures, which will take an age to download. The customer may become bored and move on to the next driving school website before your very attractive but slow-loading pages materialise.

Optimising your website

Look up articles on the Internet about how to optimise your website in order to get your site on the first couple of pages of Google. This should not be too difficult for a local driving school. If you are in the early stages of becoming an ADI and you are still employed in another job, you could try designing a website now so that it is ready to upload when you start your business. Hopefully you will not have as much free time when you qualify.

Using a web designer

If you do not feel you have the time or interest to create your own website, then you will need someone to do it for you. Shop around and look at the ADI forums. You may find there are people there who will be happy to help you for a moderate fee.

Success with the net

If you want to be seen as successful and you want to develop your business locally, regionally or nationally, then a website is essential and will become more and more so as the Internet becomes the standard information tool for all households.

If you wish to expand your business, you could use your website to advertise for other ADIs, stating the standard that is required from them. Inform them whether you operate a franchise, a commission or a set fee for each client they receive from you. Say whether you provide a car or not, and give any other details.

Driving school directories on the Internet

These are quite popular with those searching for driving schools in their area. Look for the free ones. Other local instructors will be using these directories so, in order to stand out from the crowd, choose your advert with care.

Telephone directories

Our advice is to place a small box advert in *Yellow Pages* and the *Phone Book*. People may notice your driving school name as you drive by but may not be quick enough to take down your contact number. Others may hear your name but not know how to get hold of you. You might consider placing a lineage (often free) in both your driving school name and your actual name as a driving instructor in order to attract more custom – especially if you operate both manual and automatic cars.

If you are a member of an instructors' organisation, you can have your details included in their corporate advert. This will give the impression of a well established driving school.

Be careful to purchase an advert size that is related to the amount of work you want. The public are influenced by the size. They will probably believe that, the larger the advert, the better you are, and this will therefore increase the chance of them contacting you.

Beware, that the advertising rates in these directories are rather high.

Car signage

Roof signs

A car roof sign gets your driving school name noticed most of all. Show your name and phone number clearly and boldly. For example:

BRILLIANT DRIVING SCHOOL

Call or text: Pete

01999 010 010

If you can afford it, obtain a telephone number that is easy to remember. Do not use 0800 or others that cost you money each time someone calls. If the general public have any sense, they will not use a premium number that costs them more money (to find out how to cut your phone bills see Appendix 1).

Bodywork signs

Signs on the rear bumper or tailgate, showing the courses you offer (e.g. Pass Plus) and your website address, should be enough. Too many magnetic signs can look untidy and tacky. Consider how many signs you actually do need and think very carefully about whether signs on the sides of the car, which have to be quite large, are necessary.

Permanent signs

Professionally applied signs can look very attractive and will certainly make the car stand out. This will, of course, be more expensive and, if the car is used as a family car, you will always be on duty. If you show permanent signs on your car that other people or you drive on your days off, the general public will expect the driver to be dressed smartly and your car to be clean and driven correctly. Also, when the time comes to change your car the signs will have to be removed, which may, due to fading, leave a mark on the paintwork.

The more established you become, the less you will have to rely on advertising.

Personal insurance

In our opinion you need to consider taking out insurance to cover at least the following:

- ☐ Accident, health and critical illness.
- ☐ Public liability.
- ☐ Mortgage protection.

Suppose you fall ill or cannot work again due to a car or other accident. You will not have the safety net of being able to take time off on long-term sick leave, so how will you pay the bills?

We believe in having 'peace of mind'. You and your family will be happier knowing that safeguards are in place. There are many short and long-term insurance packages, and no doubt your driving association will detail some.

Public liability

Our advice is to belong to one of the driver instructor associations. Many, if not all, provide you with substantial public liability protection, access to legal help, etc.

Pensions

Do you really want to work until you drop? If not, you should think about making financial provisions for your future.

You may have come into this career late and may already have a pension from your last employer. You may also have a redundancy sum to invest, but you may still want to top this up for your future retirement.

Planning your future

Early on, set a target date as to when you want to retire or at least semi-retire. Consider the options. Can you see yourself retiring at 60 with a second pension maturing? Do you like working and keeping your mind active? As long as you are fit and capable enough to continue, perhaps you should consider working part time, even if it means giving driving lessons two days a week and £200 – £300 in your pocket to keep your 'pride and joy' on the road and to indulge in life's little pleasures.

Choosing the right pension

Choosing the right investment, pension plan, mortgage protection or insurance can be a difficult and complicated decision for the layperson. If you get it wrong it, may be too late when you first find out. If you feel you need advice, you could think about using the services of an independent financial adviser (IFA). Whereas banks and building societies will push (and they do *push*) their own products, IFAs should give you independent advice without any pressure to buy one particular product. The advice *may* not cost you anything as the IFA may be paid a commission that will cover your costs. If you use an IFA, ask about this on your first meeting.

In-depth financial advice is beyond the scope of this book, so we suggest that, if you wish to find out more about IFAs you consult the appropriate web pages on the Internet and perhaps ask your accountant for advice – can they recommend an IFA? The whole system works in such a way that your accountant may obtain a commission from the IFA whom they recommend, so bear this I mind.

Keeping records

Logbooks

Another means of demonstrating your high professional standards is to give each of your clients a logbook. The logbook should show a record of progress, problems, dates of lessons and any other relevant details.

The client's family are going to be very interested, even excited, about the driving lessons. They will be particularly interested if they are paying for them. A logbook will allow them to see some tangible evidence of where all their money is going and how their nearest and dearest is progressing.

Logbooks may well be flaunted by your clients at work or school. Other people will see what your driving school is giving to its customers. No doubt some will grumble that they do not get that from their driving instructor. Others will listen and make their choice about where they will be taking their driving lessons in the future. Laminated logbooks, with your driving school name printed on the front cover, can be purchased from the Driving School Pro's website (see Appendix 1).

Keeping a diary of appointments

A diary is essential. It will allow you to organise your working week around you and your clients' many varying requirements. Your diary is also part of your accounts and should be kept up to date and available for inspection by the Inland Revenue. Diaries and other records should be kept safe for at least seven years.

The main ways of keeping such records are either by an A4/A5 diary or by electronic means. For example by using:

☐ a hand held computer/organiser;

☐ a mobile telephone; or

☐ using Microsoft Office Outlook by which you can print off daily, weekly or monthly schedules as required.

We use both systems. Paul uses the paper method and is perfectly happy with it, and Colin records data electronically and is again quite happy with this system. Below you will find why and how each system is used. Then you will be able to decide which one is for you.

Paul's paper method

Why do I use this method? Because how would it feel to loose years of financial records? How long would it take to restore the records? I do not know and I certainly do not want to find out! So, despite backing up all my computer files on a regular basis, I am still concerned about their vulnerability. I like the idea of using two different formats to record my accounts so that, if a major catastrophe (house fire, burglary, leaky plumbing) hits one, the other (hopefully) will survive.

Another reason is that I find small handheld devices, with those tiny little screens containing only small amounts of information at any one time, fiddly and frustrating. Give me a diary any day.

How do I do it? I use an A5 diary (W. H. Smith's A5 'Week to view with appointments') where I can see the week ahead, broken down into days and hours, and the entire entered lesson times at a glance. The ribbon keeps the present week marked. A small crocodile clip (clipping the following week to the back cover) keeps the following week marked and also prevents me from inadvertently turning pages on to the wrong weeks ahead.

Entries are made in pencil (a non-stop, disposable, propelling pencil) and rubbed out if necessary.

During periods between lessons, the times and money taken for each lesson can be totalled at the foot of each day in the diary. These daily totals are then added up to give me a 'final hours and income' figure for the week. For quick identification, these final figures are highlighted with a circle. I divide the final income by the final hours to check that the sums are correct. Even when charging differing hourly rates (as long as they do not differ too much), this check sum serves its purpose.

While flicking through the diary I can instantly gather information about how my working weeks and months are panning out.

At the end of the week or month the income and dates can be transferred to my accounts software on the computer. I use the 'time' data with a spreadsheet to find out how many hours I am working, seasonal fluctuations, average litres of fuel per lesson and anything else that I may find useful.

At the end of each year I put the diaries somewhere safe in case of computer catastrophe or in case the Inland Revenue needs to check my accounts.

Colin's electronic method

I have tried them all! The trouble with the traditional book diary is that I could never keep it tidy. If it is not tidy and clear it is easy to make subsequent mistakes – as I know to my cost.

Then there is the question of deleting/rubbing out in the diary, cancelled lessons or changing lesson dates/times. The eraser at the end of the pencil never seems to work properly – it just leaves a black mark. Then, if your diary does not show the actual lesson times either in the hour and/or half-hour divisions, it needs to be written in. There might be a need to write in other times. Perhaps the diary times do not show times, say, past 6 p.m. but your lesson appointments do. It all gets too messy – especially the rubbing out!

The other problem with a book diary is that I always seemed to have sheets of paper tucked in at the back. They kept falling out or the wad ended up as thick as the diary itself. When I did need to find something quickly, I couldn't.

Yes, I had a pocket/hand held computer as well – just something else to carry along with my coat, file, ADI licence, phone and keys when switching vehicles. The palm-top computer was rather expensive and it kept crashing.

But we always carry our mobile phone. It may have a diary/calendar feature on it. But it is not a perfect solution. You will also need to answer text messages or phone calls from clients. The trouble is that the text display can be small and the keys fiddly. There will be times when you will need to answer the phone, hold a conversation and use the diary on the same phone at the same time. So, buy another new mobile with a large screen.

I use the phone's diary and download the changes every morning and evening (while on charge) to Microsoft Office Outlook on my home PC. My Nokia phone with its large screen is ideal and has never crashed over the two years of data held in it. So, I use an old mobile phone with the business number on it and use the mobile with its large screen as my diary and to hold all other information. If the SIM cards are interchangeable, then if one mobile battery becomes exhausted or the phone is dropped and fails to work, they can be changed over.

Yes, I know — we are back now to having two phones, file, coat …! but it works for me. I have the back-up on my home PC (as well as copying everything from my PC on to a CD periodically). Keeping a back-up includes printing off paper records of lessons via Microsoft Outlook each week and storing them away, as well as having the year's diary on my mobile.

There are pros and cons for all these methods. In the end it comes down to your personal choice.

Records of finances

Keep your finances in order as you go, recording and filing monthly if not weekly. It is not too much of a chore to enter your income and expenditure into a spreadsheet like Excel on a daily basis. If you do not keep up with it you will find that you cannot remember important events to the degree required. Your accountant will not be amused as they try to find out what has been happening to your money, and this lack of humour may be reflected in larger accountant's bills.

If you do not want to use Excel you can purchase a dedicated financial software package instead. This financial software will prompt you to enter the data and then lay it out on the screen in an easy-to-read format. It will also supply software tools that will enable you to display your data in graph and pie-chart form.

Our office has used Quicken software for several years, but unfortunately this is now no longer available in the UK. Look at the accounting software at Amazon.com and read the customers' reviews. Whatever methods you use, remember never to trust your PC. Back up your data to other media (e.g. external hard drive) on a regular basis.

Bank accounts

Having a separate bank account for your business is essential. Do not let your personal and business money get mixed up. Try to bank your money regularly. You can always transfer money from your business to your private account very easily either by cheque or online. Some banks/building societies now provide very good deals and free banking services – well almost. Scout around before deciding.

Receipts

Retain every receipt and always fill in your cheque stubs. When you record your business transactions, give each transaction a number and put that number on the receipt and the cheque stub. Purchase a box file with a spring clip. Place your receipts in numerical/date order under the clip. Do not forget to claim for everything that may help your business (e.g. Internet service provider, telephone, office supplies, PC upgrades and software, cleaning materials for the car and anything else that is used fully or partially by your business).

Accountants and taxes

Organising your own records will save you a great deal in accountancy fees. Do not give your accountant a box of bits of paper, cheques and your diary to sort out. It will cost you a fortune. Ask your accountant in what format they would like to receive your accounts (e.g. on an Excel spreadsheet, using Sage, etc.) and provide this on a CD or disc compatible with Microsoft or Apple Mac.). Your accountant may not require paperwork but you should keep this together in a file that shows which financial year it refers to. You may also consider completing your annual return online directly with the Inland Revenue as this will save you even more money.

As for income tax and National Insurance contributions, you will receive a demand periodically. You can now pay your National Insurance contributions by direct debit.

Being self-employed demands a great deal of self-discipline. After all, you are now your own boss with no one to nag you. Keep up to date with your work and it will not get on top of you.

6
Working as an ADI

*In this chapter we discuss your options regarding working for your-
self or another driving school and how to choose the routes and areas
in which to operate.*

What are your choices?

Do you:

☐ Wish to work on a full-time or part-time basis?

☐ Work for a national or regional driving school where you are almost certainly on a franchise scheme?

☐ Work for an existing, local driving school on a franchise or commission basis?

☐ Run your own business?

Working full time or part time

In the early days the ideal situation would be for you to keep your present job
and carry out driving instruction part time. If this is not possible, you might
consider taking on a part-time job to help you over the first few months. This
would allow you gradually to build up a client list without any external,
financial pressures bearing down on you.

If you do not have this choice and you are going to start full time straightaway,
then it will probably be better to work for another driving school until you
become established. Find out when the new, local *Yellow Pages*, *Thomson* and BT
phone books come out. It is advisable to consider the date when you intend to go
solo so that an advert can be placed in advance of your predicted start date.

Working for a driving school

Driving schools have various ways of making money through their ADIs. If
you choose to work for a driving school you will probably either be contracted
under a franchise system or a commission-based system.

Considering a franchise agreement

There are many permutations under a franchise scheme, so please consider the points below.

An ADI working under a franchise contract may pay a set amount each week to the company/owner – irrespective of the amount of work received and the total number of hours' tuition given to the clients. The company office may keep records of work provided, even your diary details, and may therefore make lesson bookings for you. You may need to account for all lessons taken and cancelled by submitting a weekly return.

There may be an introductory offer for a set period where the commission is lower. You may or may not be able to take on private work using the car provided. Cleaning, fuel and oil top-up may be at the instructor's expense, whereas often insurance, servicing, road tax, a replacement car, etc. are at the company's/owner's expense.

Our advice is to be careful. Once you take on a franchise you may not be guaranteed regular work to the amount you require. Consider how you are going to meet your personal and home financial outlays and pay the franchise. What, if any, are the 'get-out' clauses? What is the minimum time you can take the franchise for? Will you be able save enough to buy your own car to work as an independent ADI if this is your aim?

Considering a commission contract

An ADI working under a commission-based contract may be required to pay a set fee for each lesson taken. This may differ for the length of lessons. Again, you may be required to submit a weekly return. You may also be required to submit a weekly fee on a sliding scale regarding the number of hours' tuition taken.

It is likely that, under this scheme, you will have to provide your own car. Will you earn sufficient to pay off this car and all other expenses and still have enough money remaining to maintain a reasonable standard of living? To allow this to happen, you should ask for written assurances from the owner not to take on any other instructors until your diary becomes full. You should also have first refusal on subsequent new clients seeking driving lessons.

There may be other permutations and perhaps these may be open for negotiation. Ask how the owner seeks clients (via local or national advertising) and what the usual rate of new clients is in your area each week.

Working for a national or a regional driving school

Many ADIs choose to work for local, regional or national driving schools because they like the idea of receiving clients without having to advertise themselves and also not having to rely on a reputation they may not have had time to develop.

You may also be attracted by the thought of having a new car provided, but you should consider what will happen if and when you wish to terminate the contract. If your ambition is at some stage to set out on your own, you should think about putting money to one side or you could explore the costs of leasing a car.

They are likely to have a franchise contract

You are likely to pay a franchise fee per week or month. This can be expensive and you **must** consider the terms of any contract carefully.

Are they all the same?

Do not think that all these schools are the same. Some are better to work for than others. There are two major national schools, and ADIs will consistently praise one and not the other. Obviously we cannot say more than that but it would pay you to have a chat with ADIs from each company. Talk to those who used to work for the one you are considering joining.

Working for a local driving school

If you are thinking of working for a local driving school you should make sure that it has a good reputation. A driving school is only as good as its instructors. Try talking privately to the instructors before committing yourself. How long has each been with this school? How many have left over the past year? If you can talk to an ADI who has left you may find out some of the more unsatisfactory aspects of the school, but be aware that they may be a disgruntled ex-employee determined to say nothing good about the firm.

Questions to ask

Whichever driving school you are considering working for, ask the following questions at your interview:

What are the terms and conditions of the franchise or commission contract on offer? Better still, request that this is sent to you before hand. Do not make a decision at the interview. Is there a cooling-off period?

☐ Do you have to pay commission or a franchise fee for the clients you find yourself?

☐ Generally, what is the driving school's first-time pass rate?

☐ How large an area will you be expected to cover?

☐ What proportion of the inquiries is from recommendations?

☐ Will clients, who you have been specifically recommended to, be passed on to you?

☐ If you find your own clients and while those clients are under your instruction, can you remove the school's roof sign and use your own?

☐ When you leave, can the clients transfer to you without penalty? If there is a penalty, what is it?

☐ Is your contract based on you obtaining a minimum ADI grade?

Ask about any other things you may have to pay for on top of the franchise. It may pay you to make a list of questions to ask, ticking them off as you receive a satisfactory answer. This way you should not fall into the trap of being diverted from your task by a smooth sales pitch.

Are you guaranteed sufficient work?

At the interview ask them if they will *guarantee* that you will have a full diary – to the hours you want. If they do you should be careful and take a closer look at them because it may look as though they may be willing to tell you almost anything to get you to sign up. It is impossible, over a period of time, to *guarantee* something like 'a full diary'. Demographic population growth, the state of the economy, the success or otherwise of the driving school, will each impact on the availability of new clients.

Also, if the availability of new clients does start to dry up, where will you be in the pecking order? If the local driving school is being run by Fred and his five other instructors have been with Fred for years, who do you think will get the pick of the few available customers?

Areas you want to work

Make sure that you are not going to be given all the out-of-town jobs which will clock up car maintenance/fuel bills and unproductive travelling times. Cover all these issues with the driving school. Ask how the system works to avoid unfair practices. Do not forget that these are hard-nosed business people that you are dealing with. Whether you like it or not you should be equally business like, so ask the questions.

Whichever route you choose, whether you go for a large national/regional school or a local school, take your time, shop around and compare what is on offer. Look at the small print. Calculate what it is actually going to cost you and how much money you will make. Use 'what if' scenarios.

Calculating your net income

An example: what if I have 30 customers in an average week giving me 35 hours, and I cover 500 miles during that week? The franchise cost is £x, the fuel bill is £y and the income from lessons is £z. What is my net profit? When making these calculations, do not forget to include all your costs.

Motoring costs:

- ☐ fuel

- ☐ car insurance

- ☐ road fund licence

- ☐ MOT

- ☐ car repairs

- ☐ car cleaning

- ☐ car servicing

- ☐ replacing tyres

- ☐ car depreciation

- ☐ replacement car fund (if you are thinking about leaving the franchise at some stage)

- ☐ franchise fees.

Personal costs:

- ☐ association fees

- ☐ other subscriptions (e.g. FSB)

- ☐ insurance

☐ private pension

☐ accountancy fees

☐ DSA fees

☐ office expenses

☐ National Insurance and income tax.

Note : if a car is supplied as part of the agreement, some of the 'motor' items listed above may be included in the franchise fee. Check the details with the school.

Consider the following with care:

☐ Will you make at the very least, a reasonable living?

☐ What would happen if you have to pay a fixed franchise rate but then receive few clients?

☐ Is there a minimum contract term?

Remember you will still have to pay for fuel (do they provide you with a large and thirsty vehicle? - see the discussion of diesel versus petrol in Chapter 4).

Working for yourself and having your own driving school

Many ADIs prefer to run their own driving schools. They like the idea of being their own boss and of being able to organise the day-to-day running of the business in a way that suits them. Probably one of the most satisfying aspects is that you do not have anyone (apart from your clients) to answer to. You can choose which clients to take on, which geographical areas to work in and what to charge. If your driving school is a success you can take full credit for it.

The counter-arguments to working on your own are that you will have to do all your own advertising and will be the first contact when people ring to make inquiries. You will have to organise everything from your school name to your clients' records. While it is true that you can take full credit for any success, you will also have to accept full responsibility if things do not work out.

Choosing an appropriate name

The name you give your driving school will probably depend on how high you have set your sights. If you wish to run a regional or national driving school then it is probably better not to use your own name as you may find that this is already being used in other areas. Rather, give it a unique name and register this as a trade name, copyrighting the name and logo so that they cannot be used by anyone else.

As this book does not have the scope to deal fully with this subject, we recommend that you explore it in more detail at the web address listed in Appendix 1.

Choosing an area in which you want to work with care

Your decision as to which areas to cover will be influenced by the following:

□ The number of other ADIs working in the area and whether they work part time or full time.

□ Whether you want to specialise in giving tuition in an automatic car and, if so, what level of competition you are likely to face in the area.

□ The population density. Will you need to travel backwards and forwards covering small towns and the surrounding villages? How far afield do you want to travel? Remember that the time between lessons is dead time. In other words, you receive no money, you pay the travel costs and your car is clocking up unproductive miles.

□ Whether the test centre is far away from the main areas where you will be working. Looking at these areas, is it likely that your clients will be able to afford lessons of two to three hours to cover the extra travelling time?

□ The unemployment rate.

□ The percentage of the population who are on a low income.

□ If you are considering working in a deprived area, whether you will you be able to charge enough for your lessons and whether your clients will be able to have lessons on a regular basis. In the more affluent areas, driving lessons will most likely be considered as an essential item. In the poorer areas driving lessons will probably be considered a luxury and, as a result, they will be way down on the priorities list.

Undercutting the competition

How often do you see the national driving school cars in your areas? National driving schools have large overheads, so you should be able to undercut their prices and still make a reasonable profit. How many owner/driving schools do you see regularly every day? Do you see these at weekends?

Do you want to work full or part time?

Many driving instructors work part time. This may be by choice or it may be because they cannot find sufficient work for full-time employment. If many of the instructors in your area fall into this category, then you may also find work difficult. They might not get enough work because they do not receive many recommendations. They may also have poor pass rates. If this is the case, you can move in and, by using the methods we suggest in this book, build up your reputation and flourish. Their loss will be your gain.

What is your competition?

Can you pick out the 'new boys on the block?' A shiny new headboard and signs may be an indicator. A pink licence is a give away. Who is advertising in the local papers and what are they offering? If they are advertising in this way on a regular basis, they may be struggling for work. This may be because they are poor at their job or because clients are generally hard to come by. Or it could mean that they have had a large number of test passes recently. Keep reading the adverts to try to gauge the situation.

Looking for a niche market

How many driving schools in your area use automatics? If very few, then why not have some of that action? What car do they use? Is it large and old? If so, you could consider investing in a small, newer car. Use magnetic signs to advertise boldly on the front and rear that you are providing 'AUTOMATIC' lessons. On your manual car place magnetic signs stating 'LESSONS IN AUTOMATIC CAR ALSO AVAILABLE'.

Having two cars can also be a cost-effective way of managing the family transport problem. While the ADI is using one car, the partner can be using the other.

Bear in mind that teaching in both automatics and manuals takes a bit of organising. You do not want to spend your day having constantly to return to base to swap cars between lessons. Although you will try to organise your diary carefully – having separate days for each vehicle – this is not always possible, so be warned!

Deciding your lesson fees

Earlier in the book we touched on the subject of lesson fees. In the beginning, you will need to find out (covertly) what your main competitors are charging. This is easy if they have a website.

Remember that, when you receive inquiries, the usual opening question from potential clients will probably be: 'How much are your lessons?' This is only natural. If you want to buy a product you need to know the price. But unlike customers in other walks of life the people you talk to on the telephone will quite often be amazingly ignorant of what they are buying. You have to convince them that there is more to driving lessons than just the price. Try to sell yourself and your product first before answering their question about costs at the very end.

Tell them that they will usually get what they pay for. They should be cautious of instructors who are charging low fees and can fit customers in at any time. They should be wary of instructors who will not answer questions about their pass rate. They should be wary of instructors who will not answer questions about how many faults their clients receive on average when they do pass. You should tell them what this suggests about these instructors.

Why do some schools have special offers?

You should inform inquirers that they should also be careful of offers of free lessons. They should do the maths (number of lessons with an indifferent instructor times the cost per hour times the likely number of hours they will need/receive) and work out if this deal is as good as it sounds. You should also point out (especially if you are talking to a parent or guardian) that teaching someone to drive is more than just about training someone to jump through hoops on a driving test. One in five drivers are involved in accidents in the first year after passing that test. Investing in good driving instruction will help set the pupil up for a lifetime of **safe** driving.

Encouraging clients to choose you as their instructor

Inquirers should compare like with like. Tell them that instructors' standards of instruction vary enormously.

If after all this they say that they will phone you back, it probably means they are still after the cheapest. Be big about it. Tell them that shopping around is good but to remember all that you have said: the cheapest is not necessarily the best or the quickest. Therefore the cheapest is not necessarily the cheapest! A driving instructor may 'string out' the lessons and if they have a poor pass rate, you may well fail once, twice or more. This then becomes expensive with another test plus more lessons. So, the cheapest instructor may cost you far more in the end.

Try not to lose them!

Ask if they would like a brochure sent. If you have a website and they can access your information there, give them your website address before they ring off.

Tell them that, once they have rung around other driving schools, you will be pleased to answer any further questions if they ring back.

Offering Intensive courses

Not all instructors like or want to give intensive courses. Intensive courses usually mean you will have a customer, say, for about three to four hours each day for a week, or a compromise would be two hours, two or three times a week over several weeks.

Some inquirers have often not taken or passed their theory test (when you ask about this), so the pressure to book an early lesson may not be great. By the time they have purchased and read the books, practised the hazard awareness CD and booked their test, three or four weeks may have passed. To save wasted time and expense, ask them if they have a valid driving licence and can read a car number plate 20.5m away.

If they have a licence but have not passed their theory test, then preparing for both tests can be done simultaneously. You can then spread their lessons further apart without any inconvenience. Once approaching driving test standard and the theory test has been passed then, with your approval, they can book their practical test online, checking daily for any earlier dates. We suggest that, based on their current standard and the number of lessons pre-booked, you should give them a date from which they can book their test.

However, for those who have passed their theory and who are looking to pass the practical test as soon as possible, you will need to consult your diary, along with their availability, and try to match the two together. You must consider what will happen to those regular customers of yours who usually have their lessons at a specific time each week. But if your present customers are flexible about their lesson times, then this should not be a problem.

The risk element when booking a course

There is an element of risk in booking someone in for an intensive course. You must consider what happens if they do not show up and have not pre-paid in full or in part. The way of obtaining the lesson fee, for at least part of the course, is to ask them to send a cheque for 25% of the course, to be received *at the very latest* 10 days before the course starts. This will allow time for the cheque to be cashed. You will be less exposed if you can persuade them to send the deposit a month in advance.

Shortly after the initial phone call, send them your brochure showing your terms and conditions. Also included with the brochure should be a contract, in duplicate, showing the details of the booked lessons, stating the times, dates, lesson fees, etc. The contract should also make it clear that they must be able to pass the eyesight test, must have both parts of their driving licence and that the balance of the course fees must be paid in full on the day the first lesson commences.

The client should be asked to read, sign and return one of the contracts, along with the course deposit, before the start date. Inform them that, until you receive the signed contract and deposit, you will be unable to hold open the dates mentioned in the contract. This will encourage them to return the contract and cheque promptly.

Do you really want to give an intensive course?

Intensive courses can be hard work, not only for the client but also for you. If you have a particularly difficult client, whether because they find driving very difficult or you have a personality clash with each other, then up to four hours a day in their company can be very trying. There is also a school of thought that learning to drive over just one or two weeks does not give the client a good understanding of varying driving conditions. Suppose the course takes place in 'flaming' June – no rain, fog or night-time driving, etc. Nevertheless, many schools do provide intensive courses and there is no doubt that they can be a cost-effective way of teaching.

Often, people want intensive courses at the busiest time of the year. If you can find out what the client wants, however (i.e. when they want their lessons), you might be able to take them for a couple of hours, three or four times a week without too much disruption. A good compromise, perhaps!

Clients who travel from afar

If they are coming from a long distance, they may want you to recommend local accommodation. If you undertake many intensive courses you may be able to cut a deal with a local hotel/guesthouse owner.

One-week courses

Clients may inform you that they want to do a one-week intensive course and pass their test on the Friday. You will most likely be aware that having more than four hours' driving tuition at a time is very hard work for both client and instructor. There is also a large question mark over these one-week courses. How do you or they know they will make sufficient progress to take their test, in the allotted time? You must therefore word your contract carefully regarding such week-long courses if you provide these.

If you are prepared to accept one-week intensive courses you must ensure, well in advance of the test day, that everything is in place. Obtain positive confirmation from the client that they have passed the theory test. Inform them that it is their duty to arrange their practical test for late afternoon on the final day of the course. They should be made aware that booking their test in advance of the course is done at the risk of them not being ready. Three working days' notice (including Saturdays) is required to avoid losing their test fee.

It is essential that you are notified as soon as possible once they have this date for insertion into your diary. Also keep a note in your diary when the deadline for receiving the course fee deposit is due. Further, these clients must be prepared to pay (in cash) for more lessons if it is apparent they will not be up to test standard by the end of the course.

Finally you must make it crystal clear that, if they are not ready in time, you will not take them for their test. They book lessons and their test on this understanding. Remember again that all the above should be included in your terms and conditions and in the contract that is signed.

Confirming the course and payment

Put a note in your diary so that, 10 days before the course, you ring the client to confirm that you will be meeting them at the appointed time and place. Have they paid the deposit? Remind them that you will need to see both parts of their driving licence and that the balance of the course must be paid (preferably in cash) before the course commences. Also remind them that you will have to carry out an eyesight check, so they should, if necessary, bring their glasses.

Guaranteed passes

Some members of the public may have read or heard about 'Guaranteed passes on intensive courses!' How can anyone guarantee that a client will pass at the end of an intensive course? What often happens is that, should the client fail the test, then the next test is paid for by the driving school. How can they afford that? Do they cover this by adding extra lessons or charging more? Do they make sure their clients are at a very high standard of driving? Do they work on the basis of 'Some they win and some they lose'?

Offering Pass Plus courses

These courses were introduced by the DSA to improve the driving skills of people who have recently passed their driving test. The course can be completed within six hours, at which point, if satisfied with the client's progress, the ADI completes and signs a form which is then sent off to the DSA, who will forward a Pass Plus certificate directly to the client.

The syllabus includes:

☐ town driving;

☐ all-weather driving;

☐ out-of-town and rural roads;

☐ night driving and dual carriageways and motorways.

Even the most gifted ADI may find it impossible to organise the bad weather. All the other modules ought to be covered. This means that, even in the summer, you should get some night driving in. Motorways may appear to be out of reach from certain areas, but this is such an important part of the course you could consider doing the course on a four-hour plus two-hour timetable or, if needs be, a six-hour timetable, with breaks to allow the driver to rest.

If the ADI has designed the course successfully, the new driver should find that their skills are well and truly stretched and, on completion of the course, should feel more confident, comfortable and safe in all the varied driving environments. The added bonus is that many insurance firms will give a discount to drivers who have passed this course.

The fees you charge for Pass Plus should be more than your standard hourly rate. This will reflect the fact that you will use far more fuel per hour and also take into account the extra office work you will be required to undertake and the overtime required to carry out the night-driving module.

To become a Pass Plus instructor, you will have to contact the DSA and buy the Pass Plus pack from them. More information about the Pass Plus and how much it costs can be found on the DSA's website.

7
Dealing with a new client

❛In this chapter we discuss how you can promote your professional image and reputation when dealing with your clients.❜

Preparing for your first contact with the new client

You should be well prepared when potential clients contact you by telephone. They will not want to be kept waiting on the telephone as you scrabble around making apologetic noises. Not only will this be annoying for them but they will also be receiving signs of an unprofessional and disorganised office. These potential clients may start worrying that they are ringing the wrong driving school before your sales pitch has even started.

Having equipment ready to hand

To avoid this situation make sure that you have the following items available:

☐ Pens and pad.

☐ A telephone response form (see Appendix 1). This form is, in effect, a list of questions that you ask the client. By the time you have worked down the list you should know all the relevant information about your client. Make sure that the first two questions cover their name and telephone number. If the caller then runs out of telephone credits you can call them back before they have chance to cool off or change their mind.

☐ Up-to-date information about the costs of your driving lessons and any current discounts.

☐ Your diary and a calendar.

☐ Up-to-date information about test fees.

☐ The DSA's website and address and the telephone numbers for theory test applications.

☐ The theory test postal application form to include with your brochure. Some clients will not have credit/debit cards, so they may need to apply by post. Theory and practical test forms should be available at the DSA test centre.

☐ Up-to-date information about the driving licence (foreign drivers, ages, special provisions for holders of a full motorcycle licence, etc.).

☐ A local street map and area map for out-of-town callers.

Diary calculations

If you are a successful driving school and follow the advice in this book, you may not be able to take on new clients straightaway. You will quite often have a full diary and may need to delay taking on new clients for several weeks. As clients pass their tests, places will become available. If your new client is prepared to wait they will want a definite start date for the future. If this calculation is done on the back of an envelope, it can become a nightmare. The consequences of getting it wrong and ending up with more clients than you can deal with are a potentially serious problem.

Using a spreadsheet

One of the best ways of calculating client movements is by using a spreadsheet (see Appendix 1 for the Driving School Pro spreadsheet). Information about clients' names, test dates, number of hours each client has done, joining dates of new clients, telephone numbers – in fact, any information you like – can be added to the spreadsheet. This data can then be colour coded for clarity. Very importantly, the spreadsheet should also calculate how many hours you will be working each week.

If you want to use the Driving School Pro spreadsheet, we suggest you download it and then create a shortcut to it on your desktop so that it can be quickly called up when necessary. If you have never used spreadsheets before do not be put off - you will find they are very easy to use.

Download the spreadsheet to your PC, open it and then save it under a different name. Once you have done this you can experiment with this saved version. Find out what it does, how to enter information, how to organise the information and all the other useful functions that spreadsheets carry out with ease. When you have finished with this copy you can delete it because you will still have the original untouched version to use in the office.

When clients telephone, click on to the shortcut to view the spreadsheet. You may even inform your client that you are doing this to explain the short delay. This will give a reassuring impression of a busy but organised office. A glance at the spreadsheet will tell you all you need to know and will enable you to give your client a future start date.

Making the first contact: the telephone

The first contact you have with your potential client will probably be by telephone. *Professional courtesy begins here*. On answering the call let them know, in a friendly and interested tone, who you are and what you are (e.g. 'Good morning. This is David Smith, driving instructor at Driving School Pro'). Listen to what they have to say first and understand their needs. If you can, show a little humour.

Dealing with the younger caller

If it is a young person calling you should bear in mind that they may have had a difficult time at school and/or with their parents. They may be apprehensive about another teacher/adult figure coming into their lives. Be friendly and reassuring and, apart from anything else, they will most probably be slightly to extremely anxious about learning to drive a car.

Dealing with the parent

If you are talking to a potential client's parent, try to come across as a friendly, firm, nose-to-the-grindstone sort of person. They may be paying for the lessons and they will want to know that their money is being used wisely and not being squandered as you spend 15 minutes every lesson discussing with their offspring United's chances of winning the FA Cup or who should be kicked out of the Big Brother House.

If you give the impression to your caller that you are only interested in signing them on for their money or treat them sharply or talk down to them, then you should not be surprised if they give an excuse to call back later – and you should be even less surprised if you never hear from them again.

The sales pitch

There are few statements truer than 'first impressions count'. You have a short space of time to prove to the potential clients that you are not only the best and most professional driving instructor for them but that you are also a rather pleasant and approachable human being.

If you want to look at the first contact situation in a strictly business sense, you should recognise that one telephone call dealt with successfully will mean, on average, £800-£1,000 eventually being delivered to your business account. Conversely, one phone call dealt with inadequately … well, you can probably work out the rest!

Closing the telephone call

At the end of the telephone conversation confirm your information by reading back to the client their exact address, telephone number, where you are going to meet them and at what time and on what date. If their telephone number is a mobile, ask them to have it switched on on the day of their lesson. Then, if for any reason you are delayed, you will be able to inform them why.

Ask them to let you know as soon as possible if anything prevents them having their lesson. Reassure them that it is only in the diary in pencil and can soon be changed to another day. If the date is weeks ahead, tell them you will contact them a couple of days in advance of that date to confirm they can still make their lesson. Remember to inform them of your cancellation/change of lesson date terms (e.g. 48 hours' notice is required).

Making the second contact: the doorstep

It is a good idea to have either a newsletter or brochure and your business card with your photo ID on it to deliver to your new client so they receive it before the date of their first lesson. It is also a good idea to deliver these by hand on their inquiry day as it may sway them to book lessons with you rather than with someone else. It will make them feel special, that you care about them and that they are not just another inquirer/client. Remember that every positive move from you may well be talked about among family and friends. This type of publicity is very important in building up your *good* reputation.

Knock on the door and introduce yourself. Look smart, be confident, look them in the eye and be pleasant. If this business takes place during another client's driving lesson you should first ask your client if they mind; otherwise they may see it as just a little bit cheeky to use their time/money for your business calls. Reassure them that you will put five minutes extra on the end of the lesson to compensate for the time.

Establishing the terms and conditions

The information given to the inquirer should include your terms and conditions. The terms and conditions letter should be supplied in duplicate so your client can sign one copy and, ideally, return it to you before their first lesson, keeping a copy for themselves. If the client is under the age of 18 then their parent or guardian should counter-sign. If these terms and conditions are returned before the first lesson and they cancel without giving you due notice, you could insist on payment because this has been made clear in the covering letter and on your business card.

The terms and conditions should also remind the client that they must have *both* parts of their driving licence available for inspection on the first lesson and that they will need to read a number plate from 20.5m. It should also be made clear that, if they do not bring both parts of the licence or they cannot pass the eye test, the lesson cannot take place for legal reasons but that the lesson fee is still due.

Making the third contact: the lesson

You should always aim to be punctual. This is especially important on the first lesson. Be realistic about travelling times between lessons, making adjustments for times of day, holiday traffic, school traffic and anything else that may affect your journey. Think of first impressions and your *good* reputation. Being late on the first appointment will not go down well.

You should remember that this may be just another lesson in your working week but, to your client and their family, this is a very special day and it will most likely have been anticipated for months, if not years. Turning up late on this day is not only discourteous but also very inconsiderate. If you do keep them waiting your working relationship with the client and family may be tarnished for quite a while.

On the other hand, you should not arrive too early. If you do you may find that your client is in a bit of flap before you have even started the lesson. If it is raining, take an umbrella to escort your client to the car. This is that all-important personal touch again. Apart from anything else, it will save your upholstery from getting wet.

Dress and hygiene code

Looking professional

At all times be professional in your approach, and this includes the way you dress. Arriving for a lesson wearing flip-flops, shorts and little else may not only cause offence but it also does little for your image – not only to your client but also to others who see you when you get out of the car. Female and male instructors should dress smartly and modestly - the client should not receive any misleading signals.

Keeping it sweet

Now we come to delicate matters of a personal nature. We have been talking about your *good* reputation. You may be one of the best instructors in the country, but if word gets about that you have a problem with personal hygiene you will not obtain many customers.

Normally when humans interact with each other a little dance takes place. Many people may not even be aware of what they are doing, but this dance is about personal space. Most of us are constantly manoeuvring to maintain an open area between us and the rest of the population. We all know how uncomfortable we feel when other people disregard the normal social customs and insist on getting too close. As a result of this manoeuvring for space, the occasional whiff of BO or coffee breath is not much of a problem. But when teaching you will be in very close contact with your clients. Personal issues that may not be a noticeable problem in a normal open working environment may become more of a problem within the confines of a car.

So, be 'clean and sweet smelling' but do not wear overpowering perfume or aftershave - you may have your client gagging.

Other personal issues

If you suffer from dandruff, do not advertise it by wearing dark clothing. If you are a male of a certain age keep your nose and ears trimmed. Young people may find examining minutely a bushy nostril or ear from one foot away both fascinating and repellent. Either way you will not have your client's full attention.

Your hands will be on close display throughout the lesson, so keep them clean and your nails trimmed. Then, if you need to grab the steering wheel quickly you will not inadvertently scratch your client. If you visit the toilet during lessons, make a show of drying your hands when you return to the car or use hand wipes.

If you have a long, hot, working day, especially in a car without air conditioning and you cannot return home to take a shower between lessons, you should carry a suitable deodorant and a change of shirt/top in the car.

Oral hygiene is obviously extremely important. Take a close and critical look at your teeth because your clients will – whether they want to or not. If you do drink a lot of coffee or smoke, it may be a good idea to carry a mouth freshener of some kind or discreetly suck mints.

Car code

Keep your car clean and tidy. It should not look like the inside of a skip. It should not even look like the inside of the average family car, as it should be as close to immaculate as time will allow.

Odours

If necessary, open the windows between lessons to get rid of any odours from your previous client. Carry something like Febreze in the boot but, as some people (including examiners) are allergic to them, be careful about when you use air fresheners. Use baby wipes to keep the steering wheel, gear stick and handbrake clean. Do not allow smoking in the car as it is now illegal. It is also a legal requirement that you should have a no-smoking sign displayed.

Seats

If your car does not have air conditioning, it might be a good idea to use a beaded seat cover on the driver's seat. This will keep the seat dry for the next customer. If you use one on the passenger seat, remove it before tests because examiners may refuse to sit on them. (Examiners claim that if the car has to stop suddenly, they may slide under the seat belt.)

Some instructors buy cars with leather seats because they are easier to keep clean and hygienic with a wipe over with a medicated wet wipe, but these seats can become very hot and sweaty in the summer, particularly with very nervous clients.

Maintaining professional standards

Safe conversation

Be totally professional during the lessons. Never use bad language. Never give offence or alarm by indulging in innuendo, flirting or suggestive jokes. This is especially true when dealing with young people. Probably the best way to gauge this is to imagine that the client's parent is sitting in the back seat listening to your conversation.

Be careful about what you say. No doubt you will have views about various matters and you may debate these points at home or in a pub where you know your audience. But airing your views and prejudices during lessons could backfire. Even if your views do not bother your client, they may go home after the lesson and repeat your remarks, and probably out of context. Third parties may take offence.

Physical contact

Apart from a brief handshake on the first meeting, never touch your client. For example, when buckling the seat belts let your client go first so your hands do not meet. If you touch the client by accident, a quick 'sorry' may be in order.

Occasionally clients can become emotional. If they start to cry, be sympathetic but on no account should you touch them, whether it be by holding a hand or by giving them a hug. This kind of action can very easily be misconstrued, especially if a parent or spouse hears about it later on or if you are seen doing this by another member of the public, their parent or a prospective client.

If you use your car with its driving school signs and you give your spouse a lift, take care not to kiss them goodbye. A member of the public who may have been considering taking lessons with you may not know it is your partner. Is this the way you usually say goodbye to your clients? Word will soon get round, whether it was innocent or not.

Dealing with payment problems

Being firm

You must be firm when dealing with payments and you should be prepared to deal with any money-related problems straightaway. Do not let back payments mount up. The fee for one missed lesson may look quite acceptable but, if you multiply this fee by five, you may be looking at over £100. This then starts looking like very serious money indeed, especially as it will be for lessons that have already taken place.

You should be polite and sensitive, but money problems definitely need to be addressed at the very beginning. Apart from anything else, you cannot afford for the word to get around that you are a soft touch.

You must also be consistent. You cannot be hard with client A and more accommodating with client B. They may know each other and you may have to try to justify your inconsistency.

Generally, always be friendly but firm. You will be respected for it.

Dealing with non-payments

It should have been made clear in your terms and conditions that payments must be received at the beginning of each lesson. If your client arrives without the money, you will then have four possible courses of action.

The first way is to refuse to take them on the lesson. This way you may end up not being paid and may also loose the client as well.

The second way is to ask them to sign a form stating that they agree to pay for this lesson plus the fee for the next lesson at the start of the following lesson or within 10 days if another lesson is not imminent.

The third way is, if you feel the previous two methods are a bit heavy and that you can trust your client 100%, that a verbal undertaking may do – but be very careful as many of us have been disappointed with the results of misplaced trust.

Finally, you might ask them if they have a bank card they can use at an ATM machine.

It cuts both ways

Remember that penalising clients either for late cancellations or for not turning up works both ways: if you seek payment for loss of lesson fee because they cancelled late, then you must also give them a comparable reduction if you have to cancel a lesson at short notice or give them a shortened time. State this in your terms and conditions.

Signing the terms and conditions

As mentioned above, at the beginning of the very first lesson, the client should provide you with a signed copy of your terms and conditions, showing that they understand and agree with them. If the client is under 18 years of age, then their parent or guardian must countersign this and the client should keep one copy. Although unusual, if for some reason you need to take legal action against your client, having this signed document will help your case.

Complying with legal matters and dialogue

Legal obligations

Before you attempt to drive your client anywhere, you should first check they can read a vehicle number plate from 20.5m and that they have both parts of their driving licence with them. Check their details, including their photograph.

Pre-lesson dialogue

It is important to discuss the following issues with your client. You can do this on the way to the driving site and/or when you arrive there:

☐ Ask them if they have had any previous driving experience. If so, establish exactly what that experience consisted of.

☐ Ask them if they have taken the theory test.

☐ Inform them about the two tests – what is involved, what is expected of them and where they take place.

☐ Inform them that they need to pass the theory test before they can book their practical test and that they can prepare for and take their theory test at anytime before or while they are taking their practical course.

☐ Ask them if they know how to prepare for their theory test. Recommend books and CD- ROMs to them and insist that they buy the Highway Code *and read it*.

☐ Tell them that there is no guarantee that everyone will pass the theory test the first time. Do not let them be complacent about it. Tell them about the near-geniuses you have taken in the past who failed their theory test. To avoid driving course disruption and driving test delay, advise them that they should get the theory test out of the way as soon as possible and at the latest before 20 hours of instruction have elapsed.

□ Ask them if they feel they may have any problems learning to drive. We are talking about learning difficulties here, but be very careful and sensitive about how you ask this question.

□ Ask them if they have any disabilities that could affect their driving.

□ Ask them if they are on any medication that could affect their driving.

□ Ask them if they have consumed more than the legal amount of alcohol within the last 24 hours and inform them that you have a zero tolerance to anyone taking drugs (including prescribed or over-the- counter medication) 24 hours prior to each lesson that could affect their driving.

□ Ask them whether they will be having driving practice with friends or family. If this option is available, you should actively encourage it but suggest that they wait until they have at least practised roundabouts with you before they do so. Warn them that whoever is taking them out may feel very nervous and anxious and this may translate into a few sharp words.

□ Give them some guidance on approximately how long it takes an 'average' client to achieve test standard (rule of thumb: 2–2.5 hours for each year of a client's age). The DSA carried out a survey in 2005 whereby hundreds of successful driving test candidates were asked about their driving experience. The result showed that, on average, 35-45 hours of driving instruction had taken place, along with the use of a private car outside driving lessons.

□ Tell them that they can ask as many questions as they wish, especially if they do not understand something that was covered on a previous lesson and they are hoping this problem will just go away – because it will not.

□ If later during the course you find your client is having major difficulties with co-ordination and clutch control, you should discuss with them the alternatives that are available. You must talk this over and allow your client to make the decision whether to persevere with manual or try driving an automatic geared vehicle.

Documentation and training resources

Documenting your client's details and progress

It is, of course, essential that you record your client's details. This will be an excellent opportunity to demonstrate your professional approach. If you log on to the Driving School Pro website (free downloads) you will find all the documentation you will require. This system has been tried and tested over many years by the school's instructors. As mentioned on the web page, you should consider investing in a zip-up conference folder with a four-ring file inside. You can then place the downloaded documents in this folder.

You will find that these downloaded documents will not only enable you to enter the client's details but also allow you to record their progress through the driving course. If you invest in the Driving School Pro logbooks you will have the whole package. You will also find on this web page question papers to be printed off and presented to your client at the end of lessons (see Appendix 2).

Using reliable training resources

If you have invested in the Driving School Pro graphic briefings, you will be able to start using them on this first lesson. Your client will again be impressed by your professional approach and commitment to delivering a first-class lesson, and you will be confident that you have missed nothing out.

Losing clients; some common reasons

Perceived lack of progress

One of the most common reasons for clients changing driving instructors is that they are not satisfied with their progress.

There are several reasons for this:

☐ The instructor may not have identified the driving problems and helped the client rectify them.

☐ It may be because the instructor is stringing out the lessons by sitting on the side of the road for too long.

☐ It could be due to too many lengthy intervals between lessons or that clients are not being worked to their full potential.

☐ It could be that clients are not pleased with the distractions or breaks in their driving, such as fuel stops, answering the telephone, comfort breaks and so forth occurring too regularly.

Most clients will want to achieve test standard as soon as possible, but some will be extremely unrealistic about when that date should be. Instructors sometimes come under a lot of pressure to put these clients in for the test before they are ready. You not only have your personal reputation at the test centre to protect but you also have a moral obligation only to enter clients for the test when you think they will not only pass but will also be safe, competent and independent drivers. You should point this out to them, as well as to their parents where appropriate.

At this point they may seek another instructor in the hope of being put in for the test earlier than you are prepared to accommodate. To give your clients a more objective view of their driving, give them a mock test so that they can see the type of faults – both minor and serious – they are making when no assistance is being provided by you.

Personality clash

On rare occasions the chemistry may not work between client and instructor and both parties will be aware of this. Some might not like the differences in age or attitude between client and instructor. We cannot please everyone – but we have a duty to try. The ultimate decision remains with the client. If a client leaves it is probably in both parties' interests.

Other reasons

Other factors may also cause clients to leave. It could be they have financial problems, are having domestic problems or they may just dislike the car. We must not forget that, although rare, some people are just not cut out to drive, and every lesson is going to be an uphill struggle for them. It is sometimes easier to blame the instructor rather than face up to this fact.

Arranging lessons with family and friends

Starting with a 'clean sheet'

Ideally, clients should start their lessons with an ADI so that there will be no pre-learnt bad habits to correct. Nevertheless a short period of time spent with family or a friend, just learning how the clutch works, can be beneficial. The more common faults that clients tend to pick up from private lessons with well meaning family and friends are poor steering technique, lack of mirror use, poor anticipation and poor general observation. Experience shows that clients who start with 'a clean sheet' will learn quicker and will retain information better.

Advising on when to start 'private practice'

During the first meeting with the new client, you should find out whether the client will have private lessons with friends or family. If you download the 'Clients' details' sheet from the Driving School Pro website, you will see that this point is covered when you take details from your client on the first lesson (see Appendix 1).

Our strong recommendation is to advise them not to practise between lessons until they have established good driving techniques and are confident they can deal with awkward and possibly dangerous situations. We therefore suggest that you ask your clients not to have this extra practice until you both agree that they are competent in emerging from junctions safely and are able to negotiate roundabouts confidently. Make it clear that you fully support and encourage the idea of private practice after completing these topics with you.

Problems with 'private practice'

Practice sessions with others can sometimes undo the good work you and your client have put in, and a near-mishap could seriously knock their confidence. Explain that you know they might want to pass their test in the shortest time possible but that, if the methods from others conflict with yours, it will take them longer to reach test standard. You appreciate that others have 'best intentions', but it may have been a long time ago when they took their test and bad habits may have developed. It is therefore vital that, when the client is driving with friends or family, the client insists on driving in the way they have been taught by their instructor.

If there is any serious conflict, then you should be informed. You need to know if your authority and good work are being undermined. It may help to explain why things are not going quite so well as you would expect.

Private practice near to the test day

As clients approach test standard and you feel there may be a problem if they suddenly take up 'private practice' in another car, you might suggest that they refrain from driving in another car at this stage as it may feel very different. It may have an indicator on the opposite side, it may not have power steering and the reference points for manoeuvres may be dissimilar. You do not want last-minute difficulties that might cause your clients to feel even more anxious about their imminent test date.

Concluding the first lesson

Prompting feedback

At the end of this first lesson ask the client what they thought of it. Was driving more, or less, difficult than they imagined? If they have found it easier, then this may be due to your excellent instruction and, of course, Graphic Briefings! Had they enjoyed it? Do they want to ask any questions? Are they happy to continue with you? If they are, then this is the time to get the diary out to commit them to the next lesson.

Discussing future appointments

Upon completion of this first lesson, you must state that you will always endeavour to be punctual for each lesson, but that circumstances such as traffic delays may cause you to be late. If you are to be more than, say, 10 minutes late, state that you will contact them (remind them to have their mobiles switched on). This information should also be in your brochure and terms and conditions.

If you turn up late you cannot assume that your client will be able to over-run the allocated finish time. If they cannot, another appointment time will need arranging – perhaps with some reduction in lesson fee or addition of time to compensate them. This goes a long way to show your professional approach and to gain future clients by way of recommendations.

8
Structuring your lessons

In this chapter we describe how to assess your client and how to deal with clients who have had driving lessons previously.

Two-way assessment

The first lesson is, in many ways, the most important. You will have the opportunity to demonstrate your professional approach, credibility, calmness and enthusiasm while, at the same time assessing your new client. Do not forget that simultaneously, your client will be assessing you: your style, your lucidity and how efficiently you deliver the lesson.

They will, no doubt, have heard about impatient and bad-tempered instructors. The client will want to be assured that you are not only going to teach them to drive in the shortest time possible – that they will make good progress by the end of each lesson, so gaining more confidence in themselves and in you – but also that the driving lessons are going to be a pleasurable experience.

What has the client learnt?

At the end of the first lesson the client will most likely ask themselves:

☐ How much have I learnt today?

☐ Did I feel safe?

☐ Did I enjoy the lesson?

☐ Can I tolerate this instructor for the duration?

☐ Am I likely to pass with them at the end?

☐ Are they trustworthy?

☐ Was the lesson good value for money?

Building good relationships

As a professional you will quickly have to establish good working relationships with all kinds of people who have different lifestyles, manners, language and attitudes.

From the first lesson you will not only need to build up a rapport with your client but also to build a personal profile of your client's personality and their ability to learn the skills of driving. From the very first moments you should be developing a bond with your client so that they quickly learn to trust you and have faith in your expertise. This bond should help them feel comfortable when in close proximity to you.

Employ the usual conversational gambits to build up a good rapport between you both, injecting a suitable sense of humour when you can. Talk about the weather, try to discover some mutual interests, ask them about their job or college but, obviously, do not touch on anything of a personal nature. You should be careful when asking about their parents. You should not assume that every young client has both a mother and father living at home. Questions based on wrong assumptions may engender feelings of embarrassment and pain.

Motivating clients

You will occasionally come across clients who just don't respond to conversation for a variety of reasons. They could be very shy, they may not be used to talking to an adult or they could just be rather introverted. The quiet ones can be hard to teach, especially if every comment or question has to be teased out of them. You may also find it difficult to motivate them.

It is possible that the driving lessons have been paid for by their parents (or a relative), but their son or daughter has no real interest in learning to drive. The consequence of this is that the lessons may become protracted. If, despite your best efforts, these clients continue to make very poor progress, you may consider contacting their parents. It is they who may eventually query the length of time it is taking for their son/daughter to reach test standard and the seemingly large amount of money they are spending.

Very often the opposite is true. Those who do want to learn to drive and who are paying all or part of their lesson fees are usually well motivated and tend to pass much more quickly.

Clients with strong characters

You should also consider whether your client will mind you being the dominant figure. In the early days of giving instruction one of the authors of this book had a female client who was a very dominant businesswoman and who could not get used to the fact that she was in the learning seat, being 'told' what to do and how to do it. It was discovered later that he was her third instructor. We wonder whether she actually ever took her test. You will occasionally find that some women just do not like taking instruction from a male, and vice versa. Generally speaking, you will find that the younger the client is, the less chance there is that this will be a problem.

Establishing the client's driving experience

You should quickly establish whether your client has or has not driven before. If they tell you that they have driven on the roads before, ask some searching questions to test their claims, their depth of knowledge and whether the methods and routines they have been taught correspond with the way you will teach them.

For example, ask them how they would carry out the M-S-P- S/G-L routine. What gear would they anticipate using when emerging right on to a busy road? What should they do before signalling to turn a corner, or which mirror would they use just before turning right from a major road into a minor road?

If they have had driving lessons in the past from an ADI, you should inquire as to how many lessons they had and how long has it been since their last lesson. You should ask what subjects the instructor covered (e.g. roundabouts, manoeuvres or overtaking). What was the last subject? Did the instructor use a logbook? If so, do they have it? Generally, did they have any specific problems with their driving (for example, steering or clutch control)? Ask also if they have been/are receiving any private tuition from friends or family. If they have, they may have been taught their bad habits.

Establishing the facts for yourself

You should bear in mind that what they tell you may not be completely accurate. Some will have a very inflated opinion about their ability as a driver. Others will be extremely modest and the subsequent drive will probably be a pleasant surprise for you.

If a client has recently moved into town from another area, informing you that their last instructor told them that they are close to test standard, initially take this with a pinch of salt. This may be true but it could have been five years ago. Some instructors may give a departing client an unrealistic, glowing report in the knowledge that they will not be seeing them again.

Some may say that they have had about eight lessons and have covered everything. Really? Do they really know everything in detail? It is probably better to accept quietly what they say without question and give them your assessment of their driving standard a little later, supporting your comments but without deflating their confidence too much.

Do state the good aspects of their driving, so giving a balanced view, but with them being quite clear on the work still to do. No doubt, if their last lesson was some years ago, you can qualify your remarks by stating that standards and expectations have increased significantly since then.

Assessing your client and making all necessary checks

Assessing and checking your client relates to:

☐ their licence. Is it valid?

☐ their eyesight. Check by asking them to read a number plate in good visibility at the correct distance.

Now ask whether:

☐ they have any disabilities that could affect their driving;

☐ they are on any medication that could affect their driving ability;

☐ or not they have consumed more than the legal amount of alcohol within the last 24 hours. State your policy on this. If they do not already have one, give them a copy of your terms and conditions to read later and to return signed, at their next lesson; and

☐ they have had any previous driving experience.

Acting on information received

You can now decide whether you should drive them to a nursery route, to an intermediate route or whether you can let them drive straightaway.

The client with previous experience

If you believe that their previous experience is sufficient, ask your client if they are confident to drive from here or whether they would like you to drive to a more suitable area. Some may not want to be seen by friends, relatives or neighbours making such mistakes as stalling as they drive away.

A word of warning. No matter how much of a glowing report they give themselves, if the area where you met them is on a busy and complicated road, you should insist on driving them somewhere quieter. You can always explain (quite rightly) that all cars are different from each other and you just want to give them a little time to settle, in a quieter location. Use this driving time wisely, perhaps giving your client a commentary on how you are driving (e.g. all-round observation before and while moving off; the M-S-P-S/G-L routine; and the way you change gears).

Building an appropriate rapport with your client

You might have to use the first period of this lesson to establish your authority. Your client's previous instructor may have been weak or disinterested and your client may be used to doing things their own way. Start as you mean to go on. Remember, you have overall responsibility to ensure safety to yourselves and other road users.

Do not be bombastic but just quietly insistent. It should be obvious to your client that you are the person controlling the lesson and that they will be driving in the manner you want them to drive. If there is any dissent you should reaffirm to your client that your ambitions are to turn them into a safe driver, driving to a very high standard in order to pass their test in the shortest time possible and, hopefully, the first time. The way to do this is for them to follow your instruction. This is how it has worked with all your previous successful clients.

Before they do anything further, you should point out where all the controls are in your car. Older cars from the Far East, for example, may have indicators on the right–hand side of the steering wheel. Once that has been covered, they can then carry out the cockpit checks. If you have any problems with the way they do this, you must correct it immediately and give the reason why.

Once the cockpit checks have been completed, you should now consider allowing them to move off with all safety checks in place.

Driving to impress you

You should stress that your client will not impress you by driving fast, changing gear quickly, using one-handed steering and so forth. You should state that you are looking for a smooth textbook ride to assess their safety routines, accuracy and skills.

Ask them to drive off when they are ready. Tell them that you will be watching for the appropriate method and that, after a short while, you will be asking them to stop to talk to them about any corrections that need to be addressed or to confirm their good technique.

Identifying mistakes

If they do make some elementary mistakes (for example, stalling or forgetting to carry out the blind-spot check), be sympathetic. Tell them you fully understand how difficult it is for them with you apparently watching their every move and the fact that they are at the same time having to adjust to a new car. As your client drives, you will be assessing whether these mistakes are a result of nerves or a lack of understanding of good driving practices.

If they drive in a different manner from the way you teach, you will have to decide what to do. If it is just different but acceptable, you may feel that you can live with it. But if it deviates from what you consider to be good and safe practice, you must correct it.

You will have to be diplomatic about this. It must not sound like one ADI contradicting another. This would look cheap and unprofessional. Explain that all ADIs have their own way of doing things. Your client will perhaps know this already, and perhaps this is why they have changed to you. You know your methods work because clients pass their test when they use them, and you would be a lot happier if your client readily adopts these new ideas.

Explain why you are not happy with the way they are doing things at the present. Illustrate your reasoning with hypothetical scenarios using their method and the possible consequences, compared with your methods that will avoid these pitfalls.

Building confidence in your client

If everything goes well, with a good cockpit check followed by a good move off and car control, then you should praise them for this, stating that you will not be asking them to stop just yet. On the other hand if things do not go well then you must stop to make the necessary corrections before the list becomes too long and depressing.

If you discover a great many driving faults on this first meeting, it may well be counterproductive to mention them all at this time. If you do, your client's confidence will take a battering. Their loyalties may be split between you and their old instructor. They may even think that you are just being picky so that you can get more lessons out of them.

Remembering the aim of your lesson

The aim of the lesson should be to discover your client's standard of driving and to help them to develop a better, more relaxed and accurate driving style while adding more information to their knowledge base. At the end of the lesson the client must consider that they have made good progress, have a better understanding of what you are looking for in their driving and should be looking forward to the next lesson.

Further, it is important that you have established a good working rapport and that your client has absolute faith in your ability to get them to test standard in the shortest time possible and to a very high standard of safe driving.

The client with no previous experience

If your client has had no previous driving experience it will be necessary to drive them to a nursery route. You should use the journey time to question and inform them and to work on that all-important rapport. You should also make it clear that this is the first lesson and therefore it is the foundation on which the rest of the course is built. As a result of this the first lesson may involve quite a lot of talking from you, but they will definitely drive the car before the end of the lesson (the lesson for the first-time learner is discussed in the next chapter).

9
Planning lessons and training areas

In this chapter we advise you on how to plan the first lesson for the learner who has no previous driving experience and on how to develop further lessons. We also give guidance as to where these lessons should take place.

Choosing the training area: the first lesson

Choose your nursery area with care. If you cover a large area, then investigate several suitable areas in different parts of the town(s).

Your client has to get to grips with two difficult tasks, simultaneously. They have to learn how to operate a sophisticated and intimidating machine and, at the same time, guide it safely through traffic while listening to your instructions.

The area you choose will most likely be on a housing estate, although some trading estates with modern roads and light traffic on a Sunday can provide a good location. Ideally the initial training route should be in a quiet area with long, straight, wide roads where there are few, if any, cars parked. The junctions should be well marked and consist of long, sweeping corners with excellent views on the approach.

The roads should be in a good state of repair with no potholes to damage the car. Kerbs should be low so that, if the client's steering is erratic, the harm to the wheels will be minimal. However, you may have to compromise on many if not all the features mentioned above.

Lesson briefings and time management

Relationships

At the start of all lessons, explain the aim of the lesson and what you hope your client will achieve. Remember that you should display an air of authority but also of being very approachable. Be friendly but firm and do show some humour. Your client is very likely to be nervous and they need to relax as much as possible. Try to build a good bond between you right from the start.

Checks

Before you set off from your client's house, do not forget to check their licence and eyesight, otherwise you may have a wasted journey. Before you drive off, point out the dual controls to your client and ask them to keep their feet away from them. Ensure their mobile is turned off.

Health and safety

When you arrive at your destination, take the key out of the ignition before changing seating positions. This will prevent your client from turning the engine on before you are ready. Also ask them to check over their shoulder before opening their door to avoid impeding a pedestrian/cyclist and to observe any on-coming traffic before opening the driver's door.

On this first occasion, for safety reasons, you might consider holding the driver's door open. Reaffirm the reasons, for approaching the driver's door via the rear of the car and to close it with care (i.e. they are facing oncoming traffic and to leave the pavement only when safe). Inform them that, when they sit in the driver's seat, they should do nothing until asked to do so.

Tell them that their comfort is important. If they become too hot or cold they should inform you. If they need to go to the toilet, to take a break or to up their nicotine level (outside the car), they should let you know.

Keeping records

Once you have your client in the driving seat, you should take their details, including their driver licence number. It will be easier to do this from the passenger seat, as the steering wheel will not be in the way. Using the client details form (downloadable from the Driving School Pro website – see Appendix 1) will ensure that you gather all the relevant information without missing anything.

Lesson briefings

Plan your lesson with care. We recommend you use Driving School Pro's Graphic Briefings to help you cover the points quickly and efficiently. You will have a lot of information to pass on - probably just a little too much for some clients – so do not weigh them down with facts they do not need to know on this first lesson. For example, keep the instrumentation briefing short and simple, concentrating on the bare essentials only. You can tell them about hazard lights, fog lights, low-oil pressure symbols, etc., on the next lesson. If it is raining or dark, tell them how to operate the wipers and lights, otherwise leave this until next time.

It is absolutely vital to cover the positioning of the mirrors in depth on this first lesson. Clients need to know the importance of mirrors: what they can and cannot see out of them, how to adjust them, when to use them and why. Getting into good habits at the very start, including all-round observation when moving off to cover the blind spots, needs to be enforced.

Briefing before the first drive

Once you have given your briefings and before you allow your client to set off, you should give them a little talk. Reassure them that they are not on their own: you are working as a team and that, if anything requires your intervention, you can, if necessary, take complete control of the car. Tell them that you will talk them through everything in slow time. They should act upon your instructions but they should not anticipate or pre-empt the instructions.

Warn them that, as they are now sitting on the other side of the car, approaching traffic may look a great deal closer than they are used to and, as a result, may appear to be quite threatening. You should inform them that if you are relaxed about the situation, then so should they be. If you wish them to steer away from anything you will ask them to do so in good time. If they do not carry out this instruction because they are busy working something else out or fearful of the on-coming car, then you can easily adjust the steering from your seat.

You must also stress to them that on no account must they turn the wheel quickly to avoid an oncoming vehicle. Often all they will need to do is to slow down, but you will let them know what to do in plenty of time. Steering quickly is unnecessary and could be dangerous if, for example, they are passing parked vehicles or being undertaken by a cyclist.

Managing your time

If you did not manage to persuade your client to have more than an hour then your time is going to be very tight. Although it is essential that the cockpit drill and controls are covered properly, the client will be very disappointed not to drive the car, albeit only a relatively short journey carrying out the moving-off and stopping exercises.

If you have more than an hour you should not only be able to carry out the moving-off and stopping routine (MOAS) but should also have the client drive through a few junctions. Ideally, you will have talked briefly about pull-push steering, perhaps using a dummy steering wheel to demonstrate (see Appendix 1 for a supplier). Then, with a talk-through, get them to experience turning a left-hand corner or two.

You may still remember your first lesson – making the car go forward and then stopping. Your emotions were probably a mixture of fear, excitement, triumph and then wanting to experience more. Capture and harness this excitement and enthusiasm. Aim to have your client wanting to book the next and subsequent lessons as soon as possible.

Do not forget to state that your client should ask any question they want to, no matter how trivial they think it might be. Stop periodically to praise and encourage. Ask them how they feel they have got on so far and ask them if they need a short break.

The clutch and steering briefing

Utilise any uphill slopes by having your client practise clutch control so that the car is 'hovering' on the spot, then moving slowly forwards and then drifting backwards a little (safely!) and then hovering on the spot again. Ask them to visualise the clutch plate just touching the flywheel. To help this visualisation, show them the diagram in Graphic Briefings, pointing to the area under the floor where the action is taking place. Point to the bonnet rising slightly as bite point is achieved. Ask them again to visualise the clutch plate *just* touching the flywheel.

This exercise will reinforce your clutch/bite-point explanation and help your client understand how the clutch can be used as a speed controller at very low speeds, such as emerging at junctions. Carrying out this exercise frequently when the situation allows will also help them to gain confidence in their skills and will demonstrate that they are 'masters of the beast'.

It is important that such fundamentals as clutch control and steering are fully understood and practised before advancing too far into the course. Your client should be pleased and proud of being able to control the car in this way.

Considering the time restraints

You must carefully manage your time and consider theirs. Although you may have some time to spare at the end of this particular lesson and feel you can stretch it past the appointed time to show just how generous you are, they may have another very important appointment. It is, in fact, good policy to ask your clients at the beginning of every lesson as to whether they need to finish exactly on time or not and where.

This is particularly true if you are teaching younger clients between lesson periods at school, and especially true if it is the school exam season. Younger clients may be reluctant to ask you to hurry up – even if they know they should be somewhere else. Always make it clear at the start of the first lesson that, unless they tell you otherwise, you will assume you will be finishing where you began. Otherwise, finishing elsewhere may cause you to be late for the following lesson.

Concluding the first lesson

The drive back

If you have given a lesson to a complete novice driver, at the end of the lesson you will need time to drive them back to their starting point (unless agreed otherwise) and to discuss various matters. Recap the content of the lesson and the successes they have achieved. Ask one more time if there are any questions. If they have found steering to be a problem, encourage them to practise the technique at home with a large circular plate or tray. Tell them to imagine using, or actually to use, a tea towel to dry the rim to obtain some idea of the pull-push action. This may be especially good for boys – it could be a totally new experience for them!

To help them understand, you should consider giving them a running commentary as you are driving. Point out the problems you are seeing ahead; what you are going to do next to take care of these problems; when you are going to do it and why you are going to do it. Let your client see the reasoning, logic and timing behind it all.

Ask your client if they are happy to continue taking driving lessons with you. If you are driving your client home at the end of the first couple of lessons, ask them to focus on aspects of your driving that are relevant.

If you use the Driving School Pro logbook, now is the time to produce it and explain how it works. Enter the relevant details of what has taken place during the lesson, what the lesson subject will be the next time, and before driving them home, arrange this time and date before you say goodbye to them.

Remember that the lesson continues until your client leaves the car, eagerly looking forward to the next time.

Arranging the next lesson

To avoid errors, we strongly encourage you to write this time and date in both your diary and their logbook. You do not want to turn up for the next lesson to find they expected you the day before or at a later time as a result of them incorrectly writing this down in the logbook.

While you are arranging the next lesson date, you should use this opportunity to reiterate that it is important they have regular lessons and ideally, as close together as possible. Explain that if they do this they will not lose the feel of driving: they will need a shorter time at the next lesson to think back on what and how it was achieved and that they will make more progress during the remainder of the lesson and the driving course as a whole.

At the end of the lesson, especially this first one, the client should feel they have achieved a great deal and have made good progress. Encourage your client to read through the logbook lesson notes before the next session.

Your client is perhaps your best means of advertising

Before your client steps out of the car, you might consider handing out some of your business cards to be distributed to their friends and family. Do not forget that others will ask them how they got on with their lesson. Your client should be buzzing with excitement and achievement and give a glowing report of their new instructor. Do not be surprised if the telephone rings within a few days with more clients having been recommended. It is here and after each client passes their test that your name and reputation will travel.

Moving at the pace your client can safely manage

Communication

As with most teaching jobs (and one of the authors speaks with experience as a retired head teacher), it is important that you find the right level of communication and sensitive instruction. You should get to know quickly how each client responds to your humour, briefings and instructions on the move. Adjust your delivery as necessary.

Avoiding over-instruction

Too often clients are not encouraged enough to drive in different situations where they can use and develop the skills they have been taught. The learner driver should be provided with different opportunities and experiences to deal with. It is important that you do not over-instruct. Remember, success feeds success. You should try to let go of the reins as soon as you feel your client can manage without your help.

It can be very comforting for both parties if, during every lesson, the instructor tells the client how to deal with each and every problem. At the end of the lesson they can pat each other on the back and say how well it has all gone, but this is a fool's paradise. Your client will soon come to rely on you for help, and what will happen when you are not there to give it? The examiner will not give any assistance.

The dangers of under-instruction

On the other hand, you should not push your client too hard. If you ask them to carry out tasks that are beyond them, they will probably be nervous and frightened. The lesson will be far from enjoyable and, if things become worse, they may even consider changing instructors.

Giving the right level of instruction is challenging. Look for signs of boredom or nervousness. Ask your client how they are finding things. Inform them that they must let you know if they are feeling overloaded with information they cannot handle. Clients will differ enormously in their ability to cope with the tasks presented and the frequency of them.

Gauging the client's level of understanding

When you give a briefing, look frequently at your client's face:

☐ Do they look totally bemused?

☐ Are they giving out positive body signs (e.g. nodding gestures)?

☐ Are they adding to the conversation?

☐ Are they asking questions?

☐ You should ask questions every couple of minutes - can they reply accurately? Do they respond at all?

You need to keep them alert and focused. Deliver your briefing enthusiastically, punctuated with a little humour, but do not hang on to your witty asides: your clients will become irritated if they keep hearing the same one. You may even become a bit of a joke yourself.

If you believe that the information given is not being absorbed, slow down the rate and quantity of instruction. The routes used should reflect your client's ability. If you present your client with a busy and difficult situation they are not ready for, they may panic, which will make success nigh on impossible. Putting them in this position will also knock their confidence and trust in you. As mentioned previously, if they have been really frightened they may even stop taking lessons with you.

It is vital that your client succeeds. If you believe it will help, talk them through the routines. As they develop you can ease off your level of instruction, eventually providing just prompts and questions to jog their memory. You should reach a stage where you are providing very little input, with the client dealing competently with the situations presented to them.

Pacing the instruction

Move at the pace that you think your client believes they can handle safely, but always be prepared to encourage a little more out of them and to praise them when they achieve it. Tell them when they have done more than the average person at this stage, but temper this by stating that not all progress is linear. There will be ups and downs and they should not worry when things do not go well straightaway.

What has been learnt?

At the end of every lesson it is essential that you recap the aim of the lesson. State what the client has achieved and what aspects were not quite right and need improving at the next lesson. Ask them some questions relating to the topic. This will encourage them to go away thinking about the lesson.

Remind them of any new phrases or routines they have learnt. Better still, write them down in the appropriate place in the logbook. You could add some questions that they know you will ask them during the next lesson. Ask them to look at this lesson's bullet points in the logbook later on that day or at the latest the following day. They might also consider looking at the next lesson's topic, both in the logbook and in the Highway Code, so that they will have some idea of what to expect.

If you log on to the Driving School Pro's website (free downloads page) you will find some test papers you can print off and give to your clients. Ask them to complete and return them to you at the next lesson.

Using different training routes

Matching the route to the client

The complete novice will drive round the nursery routes for a couple of lessons until basic skills are established. It will be for the instructor to ensure that their clients do not become bored or over-stretched and frightened.

Basic lessons

Until your client can control the car well (in terms of road positioning; smooth gear changing; slowing the car down to the correct speed approaching junctions; turning both left-hand and right-hand corners; good mirror checks; M-S-P-S/G-L routine; and feeling confident undertaking all this), they should stay on the nursery routes. You might consider taking your clients on brief excursions giving the same exercises on different, more difficult roads and more major roads and then taking them back to familiar territory either before or after giving lessons on emerging. This might show you whether or not they are confident and competent enough to venture on to more intermediate routes.

Clients will always be anxious about venturing out on to a major/main road, so choosing the right road and at a quiet time of day will be the next step. Reinforce the fact that they are making good progress and that driving on a main road is actually easier (wider roads, etc.). Also give reassurance that you will help them if any difficult situations arise.

This route should ideally be circular in an anti-clockwise direction to avoid the more difficult right-hand turns in busy traffic. Most, if not all, turns should be major to minor, with perhaps the majority of the route being bends.

This excursion on to the main roads will encourage a slightly different and a more relaxed steering technique around bends, as opposed to the sharper corners found on estates. This will help to overcome your client's possible fear of driving on major roads. Always talk to them, give praise frequently and help where required, and continuously reassure them that they are not being left alone to drive on a busier road.

Emerging lessons

Remember that emerging is perhaps one of the most difficult topics. Returning to familiar territory to do this will be less stressful. Any previous emerging, undertaken while delivering the lesson on turning left and right, should have been done with you talking them through the situation and encouraging them to feel and use the 'bite-point'.

After the briefings and practice on emerging techniques, general driving using sweeping and sharp corners – as well as clutch control practices on inclines – should be done in different areas. They should now be classified as intermediate drivers, and different, more challenging, routes should be sought – but avoid roundabouts and very busy roads at peak driving times. Hill starts, emergency stops and crossroads would come under this intermediate stage.

Reversing lessons

During this intermediate level you might consider introducing your client to one of the reversing manoeuvres, ideally the turn in the road. This will serve several purposes. It will allow the client to have even more practice at clutch control. You will be able to demonstrate to the client that, despite what their friends may have told them, reverse manoeuvres are not that difficult. And, finally, they will gain even more insight into how the steering works.

Many instructors, however, leave the manoeuvres to the end of the course when most skills have been practised to a high level of competence.

Roundabouts

After completing the aforementioned junctions and hill starts, the natural progression would be to deal with roundabouts. Once the client is reasonably comfortable at tackling roundabouts in all directions, the driving can then be expanded to include ever-more demanding roads and areas. This will widen their experience and help develop their expertise. Thereafter they could be classified as competent drivers.

Once the client is considered to be competent and driving with a good level of ability, confidence and independence, the remainder of the lesson topics can be covered.

Avoiding lessons in the test areas

It is preferable to keep out of the test route areas as much as possible, although this is difficult when your clients live in them. However, when these clients are able to drive quite competently, take them away from the test routes.

Realistic routes

It is important that your clients drive around as many different locations as possible to develop their repertoire of skills and to build up their experience. If you keep to the same routes and areas, boredom will set in and they may also feel anxious about venturing further a field once they have passed their test. Also, they may become complacent and believe that, because they are successfully dealing with everything in their limited world, they have mastered the art of driving.

Resisting pressure to use test areas

Very often your clients will ask when they will be driving in the test town/area as many of their friends are doing. If your clients have been learning to drive in another area, they will quite naturally be eager to get to the test area as soon as possible. It is for you to decide when it is the best time to do this. If they start using the test routes too early, they may think they are nearing test standard when they may in fact be far from it. If they start too early they may also become stale and bored. On the other hand, if they start too late they may not experience all the tricky places, which could result in a failed test.

The time spent in the test area should not be devoted just to doing 'the test routes'. Have your client drive all around the town, passing through test routes occasionally, but you do not want a client who can only drive along certain roads and is only happy reversing around certain corners.

Keep in mind that you are teaching this person to drive for the rest of their lives and that their driving experience needs to be as broad as possible. Let them drive out of their home town and into the next town. If possible, have them drive through rural areas. Use the dual carriageways. Give them navigation exercises because they will not always have you on their shoulder saying 'At the next junction I would like you to …'. They will find all this challenging and stimulating, leaving them with a sense of achievement.

Problems in test areas

Apart from anything else, there is also the problem of getting in the way of the examiners conducting tests. It could be very frustrating and annoying for the examiners to find you are practising a manoeuvre on a corner they wish to use. Imagine if every other driving instructor in the area descended on the test route at the same time!

Try to see it from the examiner's perspective. Examiners will have about 30-minutes to assess the candidate's driving on the test, which includes the manoeuvres. They may run into heavy traffic and become a bit desperate about the time. The last thing the examiner then wants is to encounter every available manoeuvring spot filled by a driving school car. The examiners will not appreciate it if your driving school name appears on the test routes too often.

Driving school cars on test routes can also be an added problem for the candidates taking the test. If you do need to use these areas, try to do so after the tests have finished in the late afternoon or at weekends. Imagine how you would feel if your client failed a test due to another driving school car causing them serious difficulties.

You should also consider the feelings of the local residents. You have to sympathise with these people. Think how you would feel if you had to pick your way through learner after learner as you try desperately to get to work on time. Then in the evening, you meet the very same problems (with the very same driving instructors) when all you want to do is go home.

To rub salt in the wound, once the local residents have had their evening meal, they can spend a relaxing evening watching driving school cars practising reverse parking around their pride and joy parked outside their house. This poses the thought that you should vary the vehicles you practise manoeuvring around and the roads you practise manoeuvres in.

There are sometimes cases on the news where local residents, annoyed with this situation, have been complaining to the DSA and their MPs about these activities, trying to shut these areas down to driving instructors.

If your driving school sign is seen too often on the learner routes and it becomes associated with anger and resentment, you may be the last on the list if any of the residents ever wants to employ a driving instructor. Do not believe that old adage about there being no such thing as bad publicity. Venturing further a field will help avoid these problems. Give your client a broader driving experience and also have your driving school sign noticed by a wider audience.

10
Preparing for the test and the test day

❝ Test day is the culmination of your client's driving course. They will have spent a great deal of time, money and effort before arriving at this stage and it is important that, as near as possible, you get it right. In this chapter we consider how to assess the client's readiness, booking the test, the weeks leading up to the test day and what to do on the day itself. ❞

Getting your client ready for their practical test

At some point during the driving course you will have to decide when your client is ready to take the driving test. This can be quite difficult to assess and there may be a lot of additional pressure on you from the client and their family.

Assessing their readiness

Assessing whether a client is at test standard is often not made any easier when their driving abilities fluctuate from lesson to lesson. At the end of one lesson you may have praised your client's abilities, for example, negotiating roundabouts. You may then find that two lessons later, their standard has seemingly dropped significantly. Also during your assessment you will have to take into account the waiting list for the test centre, which can often be over a month long. Both you and your client will also be very aware of the time taken to arrive at this point.

When you feel your client's driving is approaching test standard, consider giving them a mock test (see below). This will give you and your client a much better picture of the standard they are at under pressure, without your support.

Dealing with pressure to book your client's test

You will sometimes come under pressure from your client and their family to arrange a test date earlier than you regard to be sensible. Considering the cost of driving lessons we should not be too surprised about this, but it does make you wonder whether they have considered the possible consequences to their loved ones (and others) of them being awarded a driving licence before they are really ready. Further, taking a test too early may mean a failed test with another test fee and more lesson fees. Nothing (regarding time and expense) has been saved – in fact, quite the reverse.

Standing firm against such pressure

You have several points to consider:

☐ You have a moral and professional obligation not to put a client in for the test until you are as sure as you can be that they will not be a danger on the road. Imagine how you would feel if one of your clients, by some lucky chance, scrapes through the test and then goes on to cause a serious RTA the following week.

☐ The DSA records your test pass rate so, if candidates fail on a regular basis, your record will obviously reflect this.

☐ If your test candidates fail, they will most likely tell everyone and who their instructor is. Not a good recommendation. They may even blame you for the failure and go elsewhere.

☐ If you feel they are not at test standard but you decide to let them take it anyway, you should consider the possibility of them causing injury and/or damaging your car during the test.

☐ If your client makes quite a few serious/dangerous faults, this may be commented upon by the examiner and perhaps not in a very complimentary manner. Someone else could have taken this test slot and passed.

The importance of giving mock tests

Using the results of the mock test and considering the points above, you should be able to persuade most reasonable people that you cannot put them in for a test at that moment. The mock test results should support this, especially if another ADI colleague undertakes the mock.

If they still persist, you should point out that it is not in your power to say they cannot take the test, only that they cannot take the test in your car. If they think they are at test standard they can do it in another car, but you will not take them.

Booking the practical test

Before your clients book their test – with your approval – do make sure they are aware that:

☐ should they suffer any serious relapse in driving standard;

☐ if they do not maintain expected progress due to cancelled lessons; or

☐ if they book a test too early

you will ask them to postpone it. Reassure them that you will inform them well in time to enable them to have their test fee refunded.

Whose car will they take their test in?

Often clients ask whether the examiner's car will be like yours. To allay any worries, inform them well in advance that they will be taking their test in your car.

Making test arrangements with the DSA

As an ADI you can set up with the DSA arrangements regarding your client's test bookings. For example, if you calculate that you will require at least three hours between one test and the next, the DSA will ensure this happens. You can also request that tests do not take place on certain days. This arrangement can only take place, of course, if your client uses your ADI number when making the booking. That is why it is essential this number is used.

Booking the test date

Give your client a selection of test dates that suit you both well in advance. Make sure they understand the days you do not work. Emphasise that they must quote your ADI number when booking their test. Explain the reason why and the consequences of not doing so: if the car is double-booked for tests, the client who did not supply the DSA with your ADI number will have their test cancelled. This information should be stated in your terms and conditions and also in the client's logbook.

Ensuring they have a booked pre-test lesson

Make sure your client knows they will require a pre-test driving lesson to iron out any last-minute snags and to settle them down before the test time arrives. You must make them fully aware of the total cost (i.e. one hour for the lesson, plus one hour for the test). If there is any lengthy travelling time from their home to the test area, this will also have to be paid for.

Sometimes people quibble about being charged a lesson price while they are out on the test. They may ask what you will be doing, sometimes in a slightly sarcastic tone of voice. Tell them you will be in the test centre because you cannot do anything else. If they are even more persistent, ask them how much they think it would cost for them to hire for an hour on a test day a fully fuelled, taxed and insured car with dual controls, mirrors and L plates.

Arranging the day and time of the test

If your client lives a long way from your home or if you do not want to get up too early for the hour's pre-test lesson, then ask them not to book the first test of the day – 8.40 a.m.

If the test routes are in areas where school-runs take place, it may be a good idea to advise your client to avoid those times. Even the best test candidates can buckle under an assault of school buses, taxis, aggressively driven 4 × 4s and hordes of half-asleep children walking and cycling blindly across the roads, as well as the usual people going to work.

Knowing when your client's test is, in plenty of time

Clients should notify you of their test date and time as soon as they book it. Put this in your diary to avoid lessons clashing and ask your client to bring the letter of confirmation to the next lesson so you can check the details.

Look carefully at the appointment letter as soon as you can. Check the details. Once, when a client of ours booked by telephone, the booking clerk misheard the test centre required and instead of booking the test for Dorchester booked it for Doncaster. Could it be your fault for not checking the appointment letter beforehand?

Who should book the test?

Some instructors undertake the bookings for their clients to save any problems. Whether you think this is a part of the service you provide is for you to determine. Personally, we do not think it necessary. Give your clients dates around which to book them and the other information mentioned above.

If you do book for them there will be a great deal of unnecessary money going to and from your credit/debit card account, let alone the time you take to book them online or by telephone. You may also have the problem of the shocked client being told by the senior examiner on the test day that their short-notice test is not showing up on the DSA computer. Did the ADI book it? Did the DSA agent or computer get it wrong? Who knows? Who is the client going to believe and who needs this kind of problem?

The weeks approaching the test date

Once you have the client's test date you will need to time things very accurately. By test day everything should have been taken care of. First of all, eyes need to be rechecked because, if they have deteriorated, you will need to give the client time to visit an optician. You will need to make sure that all the manoeuvres are working correctly, that the tell-and-show response is fluent and any that other problems have been ironed out.

To help with this, you will find a form via the free downloads page on the Driving School Pro website (see Appendix 1). Print this form off and place it in the client's notes. As the test date approaches, cross off the weeks on the form and tick off the boxes as your client proves they can cope with the driving disciplines. The lesson numbers mentioned in the boxes are those you will find in the Driving School Pro logbook.

In the four to six weeks run-up to their test day, you should be giving your client several mock tests in realistic conditions. You need to get them away from the sense of security they will have become used to during normal lessons. Deliberately change your role to that of a rather reticent individual who is marking their driving faults on a test sheet and, at the same time, giving them no technical help or moral support. Slightly change your tone of voice to make it a little less friendly, and be very formal when issuing instructions.

Make sure you use the terminology employed by the DSA examiners (see Appendix 3). You will hear this when sitting in on occasional tests. This change in your delivery will most likely make your client both anxious and nervous – just like they will be on the actual test.

Giving your clients mock tests

When you first start mock tests you may be surprised by how much your client is affected. Their reaction will give you a valuable insight into how they might respond to the pressure on test day.

Just before you set off on a mock test (no sooner or they will just start worrying even more), warn your client that they may find it a bit of an ordeal and as a result, they may make more mistakes than normal. Reassure them that things usually improve markedly during subsequent mock tests.

Using a test route on a mock test

Use one of the actual test routes. Information about these is available on the DSA website (see Appendix 1). Due to parking problems you may not be able to start from the test centre, but warn your client that as you drive past the centre, you will inform them that 'the mock test has now commenced'. Make a note of the time so you can tell them at the end how long they were driving for.

You can use a copy of the actual driving test sheet DL 25 available from driving school suppliers, such as RCM Marketing (see Appendix 1). Your client will probably make errors during the drive they do not usually make.

Giving valued feedback at the end of the mock test

At the end of the mock test, have your client drive past the test centre and then inform them that the mock test is now over (making a note of the time) and that they are now going to drive to an area where you can discuss how well they did it. Choose somewhere quiet or the prearranged rendezvous point with your fellow instructor (see below) where there should be few distractions.

Before you make your comments, ask your client how they thought it had gone. If they do recognise that they have made mistakes, ask them to elaborate. This will help you judge how realistic the client is about their efforts. Asking them for a self-assessment may also soften the blow when you start pointing out where other things went wrong. By all means do let them know where things did go wrong but do it in a kindly way. They may be quite upset to discover that they have not got it all sewn up after all.

Reassure them again that the first mock test usually returns a disappointing result. Do not just dwell on things that went wrong – also praise them for where things went right, especially if they had to dig themselves out of a tricky situation. Your client's more usual standard should gradually return during subsequent mock tests.

Who gives mock tests to your clients?

Mutually beneficial arrangements can be made with other instructors whom you know and respect. The mock test can be carried out on a 'swap' basis where you exchange cars and clients. Clients (and instructors) will both benefit from this type of arrangement. This can take a bit of arranging, but it is well worth the effort.

Why give mock tests?

The first time your client experiences 'the swap' and has a mock test with another instructor, the anxiety level will rise again and more errors will probably be apparent. This swap mock test will do even more to illuminate the client's weak points while driving under pressure and will demonstrate the likelihood of these faults being made on the actual test.

Debriefing your client after a mock test

At the conclusion of the mock test the instructor should hand over the mock test score sheet and give a full debrief. You may consider writing out a more descriptive report to expand on the marks on the test sheet. Having discussed the mock test results at the end of the lesson, clients should be very aware of their faults and weaknesses at that time. The instructor and client should focus on these problems during the next few lessons and certainly before the next mock test, aiming to eradicate these errors.

Who benefits from mock tests?

Our clients usually receive two or three mock tests – one with their usual ADI and one or two with other ADIs. You will be surprised how these really sharpen the client in preparation for test. As a result, pass rates improve enormously. You will then gain more new clients, recommended by your successful former clients and their families.

Remember also that you can learn from your colleagues. Away from the client, discuss the errors they have marked on the test sheet. Listen to each other's debriefing at the end of the mock tests.

The test day approaches

Preparing your client for the car-maintenance questions

Two or three lessons before the test day go through the car maintenance questions with your client. These questions and their answers are in the Driving School Pro logbooks and on form DT1, available from the DSA website. They should be printed out and given to your clients to read.

Several weeks before you cover this topic with your client, encourage them to turn the tell-and-show questions into a home project. Ask them to involve their family and the family car. If they do not have anybody in the family who knows anything about car maintenance, persuade them to find the car manual and have a family discussion about how to check the oil, tyre pressures, etc. –

they will all benefit. They may even come back and say how timely it all was – the family car barely had any air in the tyres or oil in the engine!

You will need to spend some lesson time going through the questions and answers with your client to check they have done their homework and to make them aware of the different layout under the driving-school car's bonnet. Although this is not necessary, it is good policy to have your clients check the oil level, test a tyre tread depth with a tread-depth gauge and measure the pressure of a tyre with a hand pressure gauge. Remember the old adage: 'If I hear, I forget. If I do, I remember.'

Some clients are disinclined to put much effort into the tell-and-show questions. Boys especially seem to think they are genetically pre-programmed to know all about things mechanical and then go on to demonstrate that nothing could be further from the truth. Inform your clients that the tell-and-show Q&A (questions and asnwers) is where they set out their stall on test day. It will be the first real opportunity the examiner has to form an opinion of this person standing in front of them.

Tell your client to look at it through the examiner's eyes. They have probably had a grim day where a couple of candidates have already tried to kill them. Now they have yet another waffling test candidate who can barely open the car's bonnet successfully. How will that affect the examiner's view of the candidate for the rest of the test?

The day before the test

It is a good idea to arrange a lesson on the day before the test. This is aimed at settling the client so they are confident in their driving abilities and so they know how to respond to the tell-and-show Q&As part of the test. They might then have a reasonable night's sleep. Ask your client if there is anything specific that they want to practise.

At the end of the lesson reassure them about how the lesson has progressed. At this stage you need to bolster their confidence. It's too late now to be over critical.

If the test is booked later in the day, you might suggest that they go to work/school or do something active to keep nerves to a minimum.

Getting the documentation ready

On this pre-test day, remind your client about the documentation to have ready and available – before they go to bed.

The documentation comprises:

☐ the new-style licence (ID card and paper counterpart);

☐ the theory test certificate; and

☐ the letter of appointment.

At some stage you should inform your client that, no matter what the outcome of the test, you will drive the car back. The reason is that your client will most likely either be too elated or too upset to drive safely. It is probably better to leave out the second reason when you explain things.

At the end of the lesson, reassure them they have nothing to worry about and you expect them to pass easily.

Managing the test day

Check your car well before the test. Check the tyre pressures, ensure all the fluids are at the correct level and make sure that all the lights are working. Move all your loose equipment into the boot. This is a health and safety issue, especially if the emergency/controlled stop is carried out. You may not be able to clean the car directly before the test, but it should at least be cleaned first thing in the morning. Your car will be lined up with other driving school cars and comparisons will be made.

Be smart

You should pay particular attention to your personal smartness on this day. Examiners have to be dressed in a professional and reasonably smart manner and they may be 'old fashioned' enough to expect you to be just as professional. In our opinion, turning up at the DSA test centre dressed in jeans and a T-shirt shows poor professional standards.

The time to meet your client

Arrange to meet your client at a time that allows an hour to drive around the test centre town. Take into account the traffic conditions for that time of day, the weather conditions, road works and anything else that may affect your journey. Your client will be tense enough without having to worry even more about being late.

Welcome your client with a smile and make sure they are wearing something comfortable and suitable.

Checking the documentation

Check their documentation. Is their address correct? They may have moved during their driving course. If their address has changed, then the appropriate section of the paper licence should be completed, stating their current address. This must be signed and dated.

If you are using the driving school's logbook, have your client place the documents inside the cover for safe keeping. When they have to produce the documents at the test centre the examiner and other people in the waiting room will see how professional your school is – using your logbook showing your driving school logo.

The test day programme

Explain the structure of the driving test day:

□ You will be using the lesson before the test to have a final look at the tell-and-show questions and to practise the manoeuvres and emergency stop.

□ The time you arrive at the test centre should allow for them to relax a little and to use the toilet facilities if necessary.

Make sure that if your client has a mobile phone with them, it is either turned off or on silent. The examiner will be far from pleased if it rings during the test.

Go through the car maintenance questions. Make sure they still know where the bonnet pull catch is. It is important that you do this straightaway just in case you have a light not working, so giving you time to replace the bulb. You might consider for the same reason checking the lights and tyres visually again when you arrive at the test centre. Remember to carry a spare set of bulbs in your car and know how to change each.

The aim of the lesson prior to the test

You should be calm and should not cram everything in to this short period of time. Do not try to go round as many test routes as possible. Practise the manoeuvres early and then give your client a relaxing drive. Be positive and reassuring, calmly mentioning any errors that have been made.

Plan your journey well. You do not want to have a last-minute dash through heavy traffic to make the test appointment.

Aim to arrive at the test centre approximately 10 minutes before the test so that you do not get in the way of the test candidates arriving back late. If possible, park the car in a position that will allow an easy 'move off' at the start of the test.

Remind your client that, during the tell-and-show, they should be aware of health and safety issues. If the car is parked on a main road they should use the footpath side of the car during the checks, making sure they do not leave the doors open across the footpath.

Remind your client about carrying out the cockpit check after the examiner has explained the format of the test and has asked your client to go when ready. The examiner does not know that your client was the last person to drive the car, so the usual preparations should be carried out before moving off. It is good practice for your client to check the handbrake and to make sure that the gears are in neutral as soon as they enter the car. In effect, the handbrake is checked twice on the test.

Reassuring and building confidence to counter nerves

Give all necessary reassurances that you expect your client to pass the test irrespective of the faults made during the last hour.

Last-minute do's and don'ts

Finally, before leaving the car, remind them about observations before and while moving off. There may be great deal of activity in the area with cars moving off in a short space of time. There may be a possibility that there will be other test candidates moving off from behind or in front, just as your client thinks about moving away. Inform your client that a signal is recommended just before they do move off, having first assessed that it is safe to do so, in order not to affect another road user.

If you think the weather is going to be wet and/or dark, remind your client how to use the wipers and lights, as necessary. Make sure that the demisting facilities will come on automatically. Remember though, this is a reminder as it should have been discussed in the previous lesson. So mention it calmly.

Before you leave the parked car and head off towards the test centre, have your client lock, unlock and then re-lock the doors again, using whichever locking system your particular car employs. This may appear to be an insignificant point, but you do not want your clients to fumble and embarrass themselves at the very start of the test. As you walk to the waiting room, inform your client that you will be waiting for them on their return.

Arriving at the test centre

There is a great deal to be said for taking the client to the test centre well before their test to have a look round and to find out where the facilities are. However, time and distance might not allow this.

On entering the test centre, point out where the toilet facilities are located and show them where the waiting room is. When settled, give your client your spare car key, which should be the only key on the ring. This will save them having to find the appropriate key to use when opening the car door.

Also, if they happen to drop this key down a drain while opening the car door and holding their documentation, handbag, etc., with shaky hands, you will not lose your front-door key and any other car keys. Similarly, if one of the key fobs malfunctions, you will have a back-up.

Have your client's licence and theory certificate ready inside the covers of the logbook if they have one, or out of any wallet/bag to save fumbling time. As you wait, talk to your client to take their mind off the approaching test.

Supervising examiners observing tests

Occasionally, there is a supervising examiner assessing the standard of the examiner giving the tests. Explain this to your client. This will mean there will be three people in the car. The implications of this are that the increased weight will affect the car's handling round bends, on hill starts and so forth.

If you normally remove a rear seat head-restraint, it should be easily accessible because *you* will need to replace it - the supervising examiner will want to sit safely in the offside, rear seat. Make sure that the client is aware that the supervising examiner is observing the examiner and is not involved in any way in testing your client's ability to drive.

Times when you observe the test

On occasions you might choose, with your client's approval, to sit in on the test yourself. Not only should this be done periodically but your client might also wish it. Sometimes someone being there whom your client knows can be reassuring. It is the client who must ask if you can sit in on the test.

Inform your client that you are not allowed to say or do anything throughout the test and that they must not talk to you. Sometimes you might want to sit in on a test to find out how your client's driving differs from their usual standard with you, especially if they have failed the last one or two tests unexpectedly.

Talking to your client

Periods of silence can be very stressful at this time. Remind your client about the format of the test so they know what to expect as you approach the test centre. Your briefing should be something along the following lines:

The examiners will enter the waiting room and call out the names of their candidates. Once you have met your examiner, your examiner will ask you to read the declaration concerning your residency (you have lived in the UK for a minimum of 185 days in the last 12 months) and that the car is insured for the purpose of the test and meets relevant legislation. You should sign on the line, keeping your signature within the box.

On your way to the car, the examiner will introduce themselves and will ask you to read a car number plate. On arriving at the car, the examiner will ask two vehicle maintenance questions selected from the show-and-tell question bank. Usually there will be one show-me and one tell-me question. In inclement weather there may be two tell-me questions carried out inside the car.

After this the examiner will explain the format of the test and then ask you to get ready and to move off. The area will be busy and you must make absolutely sure that it is safe before you do move off. Signal before doing so.

An alternative approach

To cover the above points and to save adding to your client's anxiety, you could think about producing a small pamphlet (folded A4) using a desktop publishing program. The pamphlet could contain the test centre information as indicated above, with other information about the test that you may wish to include. Do not forget to have the name and logo of your driving school prominently displayed.

When you decide that your client is ready for the test you should hand them one of these pamphlets. This is the kind of small but important touch that gets driving instructors talked about. The chances are that your competitors will not have anything like this. Your clients may show it to their friends at school, college, etc., and might even end up briefing your competitors' clients about the test using your pamphlet. When this takes place, other potential customers may be looking on and deciding which driving school they will be going with.

After the test

When your client returns from their test, you should be waiting to hear the debriefing from the examiner. Try to wait out of sight until they have stopped the car and switched off the engine. This is especially important if they have to carry out a final manoeuvre, such as bay parking. Listen carefully to what is being said. Remember this information, especially if your client has failed this test. This will help prepare them for the next one.

Note : due to the Data Protection Act the examiner is obliged to ask the test candidate if they mind you listening to the debriefing. On occasions the candidate may decline. If this is the case you should remain out of earshot.

Listening to the debriefing

Whenever you can, listen to the debriefing at the end of every test. Analyse the driving errors and serious/dangerous faults your clients make during the test:

☐ Is there a pattern?

☐ Are the same faults repeated by many of your clients?

☐ If so, are you covering this topic sufficiently and thoroughly?

☐ You should, of course, aim for zero faults.

Consoling or congratulating your client

Be ready either to console or to congratulate your client. You should be brief and leave the test centre reasonably quickly as the next candidates may want to use the parking space.

Always have a box of tissues easily to hand. Those who fail will naturally be upset, often reliving every aspect of the test as you drive them home. It is also a difficult time for you as their instructor. Gently probe to see what state they are in and if they wish to talk about where it went wrong. If they do not want to discuss it, you should remember that their parents will most likely want to know why they did not pass, especially if they are paying for the lessons. Let your client know that, if necessary, you will be happy to talk to the parents on the telephone.

If your client wishes to talk about it, you can gently explain where they went wrong and what can be done to rectify it. Quite often candidates are so upset that, during the debriefing, they never really listen to what the examiner is saying. Even if they have made the same errors that have had you tearing your hair out in the past, and even if there ever is a good time to say 'I told you so', this definitely isn't it.

At the appropriate time, give them reassurance and tell them they should book another test soon. Ask them to inform you as soon as they have a date so that you can enter it into your diary. Explain that you estimate that they will need x amount of extra lessons to iron out the problems found on this test.

Offering further advice to those who pass

When your clients pass, they will be on cloud nine and may want to telephone their friends and family. During the journey back (remember to drive your client for safety reasons), find time to talk about the merits of them taking the Pass Plus course.

Also ask them to be cautious about jumping straight into their car and taking it out for a drive. They will find it strange to be on their own - with nobody there to give them guidance. It would be better if they went out first with a parent and then later on their own at a quiet time of the day.

If the car they intend to drive is new to them, there will be a possibility of stalling, especially if it is petrol driven after learning in a diesel engine car.

Whatever their thoughts are about when to drive their car, this should not be done as soon as they arrive home. It would be better if they just settled down for an hour or two before picking up the car keys. Obviously you cannot dictate what they do but, if they do have an accident, you can at least inform the parents that you advised very strongly against such action. This is the kind of information you could include in your pamphlet. Then, if something does go wrong, you can point out that you had warned them about this danger.

Being at risk of having accidents

Diplomatically, tell your client that accidents occur within the first few minutes, hours, days and months of passing a driving test and particularly with those between the ages of 17 and 25, and especially when they have their friends in the car. Point out that, in the early days, it is very easy to be distracted from the driving task by conversations in the car. Make it clear that they should not be pressured by their peers into driving fast or taking long journeys. Inform them that, although they have passed their test, it will take a very long time before they are recognising, at the very best, most of the potential dangers.

Finally, remind them to keep a 'clean' licence, for if they receive six or more points within the first two years of passing their test, they may lose the licence and have to reapply to undertake both parts of the test again. Also advise them that, if they have been insured to drive another car, they should inform the insurance company of their changed status (i.e. no longer a learner).

On arrival home, congratulate them again and give them some more of your business cards. They are going to tell a great many people that they have passed and the word will spread. Feel pleased with yourself – and be careful driving to your next client.

11
Miscellaneous matters

Many driving instructors go through a process of trial and error when developing an efficient, effective and smooth working day. This chapter is really a compilation of information, tips and hints that have been gathered over a number of years managing driving schools. We do not claim that this is the only way to run a driving school or that it is the definitive way – only that it all works well. As we have tried and tested various items over the years we feel we are in a position to recommend the ones we have found to be successful.

Buying car-roof signs and magnetic signs

There are a number of companies that supply signs for driving school cars, and the signs come in various styles and sizes. Decide on the information you wish to put on your signs. Do not get carried away with fancy fonts and logos. Your sign should be easy to read in a moving-traffic situation. Above all, make sure that your contact telephone number is clear and easy to read.

Once you have decided on the layout, search the Internet for the best price (you will find some retailers listed in Appendix 1). If you have an unusual roof shape such as the Ford Ka, you may need to purchase a specific sign for that contour.

Mounting the roof sign

Before you mount your new sign, apply a protective plastic film to the roof. This film should be available from the retailer. It may well come as part of the order, but do check. Do not stick the film to the magnetic plates underneath the sign. If you do, the magnets will attract any stray metal particles, which will then stick to the film. Everyday dirt and dust will also become embedded in the film, and periodically removing and replacing the sign may cause scratches to the roof of your car.

Note: if the film comes with its own instructions, you should read them to make sure they do not disagree in any way with the following tips. We suggest that the manufacturer's instructions take precedence.

You should apply the film on a dry but overcast day otherwise the foam (see below) may dry on the car's roof before you can use it. It is important that the film is located in the correct position. Calculate where the film should be located on the roof, taking note of any obstructions, such as aerials and sunroofs. Mark the position for the film on the roof with a few chinagraph (or similar) pencil marks. Make quite sure that the marked area is square to the roof plan. Measure the width of the car roof and as necessary, cut the film to length.

Before applying the clear sticky film you should first spray the designated area of the roof using a small sprayer containing a solution of warm water and five or six drops of washing-up liquid This water/detergent solution will allow the film to be moved around the roof without sticking to it. You can either spray the liquid on to the roof or shake/stir the solution to a froth and apply by scooping the foam on to the roof.

Place the film sticky-side down on top of the foam and carefully slide it around, aligning it to the chinagraph marks. Using a small squeegee or similar rubber-bladed or plastic tool, remove the air bubbles and any excess liquid from under the sign by working from the centre outwards, making sure that all the air bubbles are removed. If you find some bubbles cannot be removed with the squeegee, carefully prick them with a pin and try again, but be careful that you do not mark the paint.

After this process, wash down your roof and car with clear water. Leave for 24 hours before mounting the sign on the car's roof.

If you need to take off the film (e.g. when you sell the car), it should be removed by first warming it with a hair drier as you carefully and slowly peel it off. Remove any sticky remains with a special remover (usually available from the suppliers of roof signs).

Cleaning the signs

The roof and magnetic signs should be kept clean. Change the sign if it starts to look tatty. If potential customers are thinking of using the displayed information to contact you, grimy or discoloured signs may put them off. Clean the signs regularly.

The plastic signs can be brought back to something like their original state by using a cream kitchen cleaner. As the polishing/cleaning qualities of these products may differ, experiment by cleaning a small area first to make sure there will be no damage to the graphics.

Magnetic signs on the sides of the car should be removed from the car periodically to clean the accumulated dirt from underneath. If magnetic signs are left on the car for too long they may start 'attaching' themselves to the paintwork, so becoming surprisingly difficult to remove.

Purchasing additional mirrors and lenses

Interior mirrors

These can be purchased from car-accessory shops and usually rely on a suction cup to fix them to the windscreen. During very hot weather the mirrors have a tendency to fall off. One solution is to make sure that both the glass and suction cup are clean. Before re-fixing the mirror to the window, apply a light smear of cooking oil to the suction cup. They may still fall off, but not so often.

Exterior mirrors

We recommend the small, fisheye lenses. These can be fixed to the door mirrors. They are usually attached to the lower left position on the nearside door mirror to aid the reversing manoeuvres. Examiners do not generally mind these being used so long as the driver does not overuse them, so neglecting all-round observations, especially the views through the rear window.

Wide-angle, rear-view plastic lenses

These can be fitted in the rear window to enable the client to see the kerb while reversing round corners. These lenses come in two forms: either hard plastic or a softer plastic that is fixed to the rear window with the aid of water. In our opinion the softer plastic version does a better job. These are available from car-accessory shops and are approximately 178 mm x 229 mm. The slight drawbacks of using these are that the rear window heater cannot be used (no problem if the car has air conditioning) and on bright days, the lens develops a slight 'flare' around it, which could affect the view.

To use the lens, mark the bottom nearside corner of the lens (a black dot, for example) and then have the client keep that marker in the gutter or on the kerb (or whatever suits your car) while reversing round the corner. A word of warning: the lens should only be used as an aid when the kerb is not in view through the rear window; otherwise the lens's wide-angle properties tend to deceive the viewer.

Cleaning the driving school car

In an attempt to judge your standards, potential customers will either consciously or subconsciously cast an eye over the general appearance of your car. After all, your car is the tool of your trade. Traditionally, crafts people have always been measured on how they look after their tools and equipment. The general public may randomly select a driving instructor, so such details may affect their decision. Even people who normally have their own cars looking like the inside of a skip may be quick to judge an ADI who has a scruffy vehicle.

Keep the car tidy. Do not have rubbish floating around and do not allow food and drink (apart from possibly water) to be consumed in the car. Your training aids should be kept tidy and secure.

Exterior of the car

Water supply and equipment

You should consider having an outside water tap with a hose connection located near to where your car is parked. If you do not have one, it is probably a good idea to have one plumbed in. Over the coming years this will save you a great deal of time and effort. A good-quality, kink-resistant hose should be used with quick-release connections. For the tap-to-hose connector use a metal fitting as the plastic ones tend to snap.

A pressure washer should not really be necessary if you wash your car frequently, unless you collect a lot of mud and soil under the car in country areas. If you do use a pressure washer you should be aware that you could damage your tyres. Use the Internet to look up the latest information on this potential danger.

Washing tips

If the car does not require a full wash every day, (for example, during the summer months), you should at least clean the windows and mirrors every morning to remove traffic grime, dust and insects. To clean the glass, use a small bucket containing a solution of water and a couple of squirts of screen wash or a proprietary bottle of window cleaner. Finish with the squeegee and chamois or microfibre cloth.

Washing your car should be carried out on a regular basis, probably every morning in the winter (as long as it is not frosty). If the car is washed this often, it should not be too much of a time-consuming chore, and you will find that shampoos and polish will rarely be required.

Use a car brush attached to the end of a hose. Do not forget to flush any dirt away from inside the wheel arches. Look out for algae growing on windows and door seals and remove.

Follow this with a quick squeegee over the windows, including the area of film where your sign sits on the roof. Wiping the windows and exterior mirrors with a chamois or microfibre cloth should complete this routine. This cleaning routine should take about 10 minutes - just time for the breakfast kettle to boil (if you have a very slow kettle).

Cleaning and checking the wheels

While cleaning the wheels you should use the opportunity to check the tyres for tread depth and any damage, including tracking damage. This can show itself by uneven wear across the tyre's width. Tracking alignment can be affected by kerbing – an unfortunate occupational hazard for driving school cars. You need to detect the problem early before you prematurely wear out your tyres.

Window seals and wiper blades

Periodically wind down the windows and clean the inside faces of the rubber seals. Dry the seals off before raising the windows. Do not forget the areas that are exposed when the doors are opened. These areas can become very dirty, and clothing can be affected especially if it gets trapped in the door.

Every so often, give the wiper-blade edges a good clean with a tissue dipped in neat screen-wash additive.

Engine bay

Open the bonnet and make sure that areas where your clients may brush up against are kept clean for when they carry out the tell-me/show-me routines.

Interior of the car

You should periodically give the inside of the car good clean, including the inside surfaces of the windows and interior mirrors. Give the floor a good vacuuming.

Air fresheners

You should not use permanent air fresheners in the car. Some clients and examiners may be allergic to them. If the air is pungent after your last client has left you, drive with all the windows down until the air is changed. If the weather will not permit this, before setting off for the next appointment, use a spray air freshener or fabric freshener spray.

Keeping lesson records

Whether you choose to record your lessons on paper or electronically, keep ahead of things and complete the records at the end of each lesson.

Security

If you use the paper method, make sure that files/folders are secured in the car. In the event of an accident you do not want anyone hurt by a heavy A4 folder, and you do not want your records scattered if the file bursts open. For driving tests, all unsecured items should be placed in the boot. Do not forget that a tried-and-tested lesson-recording system can be downloaded for free from the Driving School Pro website.

A good storage solution for paper records is the 'pilot' type of case. These cases are box-like in shape and hold a great deal of material in a very accessible way. They can often sit on the floor behind the front passenger seat. If you do use one and it affects how far the seat will slide back, make sure it is removed before a driving test takes place.

If you use an electronic lesson-recording system, keep the device in a safe and, possibly, padded place so that it will not be broken in the event of an accident or during a practice emergency stop. Remember to download the information daily on to your PC in the event the unit fails.

Daily receipts

Every time you buy anything for your business you should keep the receipt. Do not just toss them into a glove box because this will probably lead to a lot of head scratching when you get round to entering them into your accounting system. To save time later on, you should make sure they are filed in the correct order. If you have a compartment in the car that you can dedicate to this filing activity, then use it.

As soon as you receive them, file the receipts face down, in chronological order. When the time comes to remove them from the car, just turn the pile upside down and they will be ready to be copied into your accounts.

Suggested equipment to carry in your car

We suggest you carry the following cleaning products in your car:

☐ Several **cloths to clean windows**. You will be surprised how frequently you will need to clean the outside of your car windows. Try Magic cloths from Wilkinson's.

☐ **Window cleaner spray**. Try Tesco's own brand.

☐ **Baby wet-wipes** are quite cheap and usually good enough for cleaning your hands and the steering wheel, gear stick and handbrake, or you could consider using medicated wipes.

☐ **Upholstery cleaner** and a **freshener** (e.g. Febreze), as well as an aerosol spray to freshen up the air inside the car.

☐ **Car battery-powered vacuum cleaner**.

Other items you could carry include the following:

☐ **Mobile phone** for emergencies and for contact with other people (only between lessons and, of course, while the car is stationary and with the engine turned off.) Keep the mobile phone on 'silent' during lessons. This way you will have a record of the number to call back.

☐ **Beaded seat cover**. Nervous learners, who perspire profusely, can be a real problem and it will not be very pleasant for you to sit in the driving seat immediately after they have departed. A car fitted with air conditioning will help avoid these problems, and a beaded seat cover will allow the cool air to circulate.

☐ A couple of **cushions** to raise client's height.

☐ The effects of dehydration can affect concentration and general health. As you may be in the car many hours you should carry **liquids to replace lost fluids**. You should also advise your clients that they should consider bringing some bottled water to the lesson. If the weather is hot they may be kept in a cool-box or a small car-fridge. For obvious reasons, it is probably best not to consume carbonated drinks. *Note*: do not offer drinks or food to your client – it could be seen to be irregular by your client or by others.

☐ **Magnetic** or **suction-cup windscreen attachment** to display your ADI/PDI licence.

☐ Container of **windscreen wash solution**. Not only will you be travelling many miles and often in bad weather but you may also need to top up the reservoir before the test. Use the tell-me/show-me session before the test to check and fill if necessary.

☐ **Spare light bulbs** are a must. Make sure you have a spare set and understand how to replace blown bulbs. Do not tempt providence – Murphy's Law may well occur just before a test, and the test may be cancelled.

☐ A well maintained **spare wheel**. If possible, carry a normal spare wheel and not a space saver as these cannot be used for a test. Make sure you know where the jacking points are, that you have the tools for the job and that all are easily accessible. If your client would like to be shown how to change a tyre, then why not allocate part of a lesson for this? Carry some disposable, powdered latex or plastic gloves.

☐ **Umbrella** and two sets of **waterproofs** in case of breakdown (you both may need to get home without the car) or to change a tyre – remember Murphy's Law. Umbrellas can also be used to escort clients to and from the car and while you stand outside the car listening to the examiner during the debrief.

☐ **High-visibility reflective jackets or vests**. Make sure you and your client wear these when working outside the car (tell-me/show-me). It may seem a little over the top but we have to lead by example and establish good, safe practice. You could even have the name of your driving school printed on the back – good advertising of a school that cares for its clients.

☐ **Black bin liners**.

☐ **Rolled beach mat** for lying or kneeling on while changing a wheel, etc.

☐ Good **first aid kit** and **accident book** (health and safety - see Appendix 4).

☐ Details of your **breakdown/recovery** organisation and **membership card**.

☐ **Form to log details of other driver's insurance company**, etc., in the event of an accident, along with details of your own insurance company to pass on to others.

☐ **Window squeegee**, **ice scraper** and **de-icing fluid**.

☐ Stiff-bristled **hand brush** for floor mats.

☐ **Warning triangle**.

☐ **Tyre pressure gauge**, **tread-depth tool** and **tyre pump** for demonstration purposes during the tell-me/show-me briefings – and, of course, to check your tyres on a regular basis.

☐ Perhaps a **small cross-section of a tyre, valve and valve cap** to demonstrate tell-me/show-me on wet days or dark nights.

☐ **Torch** and **spare batteries** or a hand-wound torch.

☐ **Satellite navigation unit** (GPS) if necessary for demonstration on lessons or for navigation. If you do have your 'sat nav' in the car, make sure that, if you have to leave the car, you hide all evidence of its existence. This includes the cradle, and even clean off the circular residue mark on the windscreen.

☐ If you do not have a GPS unit, **local area and OS maps** to find the way to your new client or to avoid traffic hold-ups (especially on the way to the test).

That's filled your boot nicely!

Postscript

We wish you every success in your profession as an ADI.

We trust that you will have found this book to be useful and will continue to find it useful as you develop your career. Remember to keep up with the latest industry developments by using the websites listed in the appendices, and we recommend that you join your local and national ADI groups.

If you can think of any more tips or hints, or anything else you think should be included in this book, then please email them to us via the Driving School Pro website so that, for the benefit of fellow ADIs/PDIs, we can include them in future books, including further editions of this book.

Appendix 1
Web addresses and contact details

Note: the suppliers given below and throughout this book are those we have used over the years. There are other suppliers and these often advertise in magazines and on the Internet, etc.

Driving Standards Agency (DSA)

For ADI test fees (Parts 1, 2 and 3), tell-and-show questions and answers, local test routes, Pass Plus and any other information about driving instructor-related matters, log on to **www.dsa.gov.uk**.

Warning: this site contains a great deal of important and useful information that may be difficult to locate at first. Persevere and look out for the downloadable pdf files.

Driving School Pro

Sunnyhill House
Main Road
Osmington
Weymouth
Dorset DT3 6EE

Tel: 01305 832661 (message service only); 07831 841031 (urgent matters only)

Website: **www.drivingschoolpro.co.uk**
Email: **sales@drivingschoolpro.co.uk**

Graphic Briefings, logbooks, free downloads and other driving school material can be found at the above website. You can keep track of your clients' details and progress and when you will have time for future clients by using the spreadsheet available from the free downloads page at this website. The ADI's telephone response form can also be downloaded from here for free.

Driving instructor websites

Websites where you can access information, ask questions, keep up to date and discuss ADI-related matters with other instructors:

www.drivertrainingtoday.co.uk
www.ukdic.co.uk/forum/index.php

Suppliers of driving school equipment

Dummy steering wheels, driving test report forms (DL25), etc. can be obtained from RCM Marketing Ltd:

20 Newtown Business Park
Albion Close
Poole Dorset
BH12 3LL

Tel: 01202 737999
Website: **www.rcmmarketing.co.uk**

Retailers of car-roof and magnetic signs

These are the ones we use, but more can be found advertised in the various driving instructor association magazines. Your local sign maker may also be to supply one (see *Yellow Pages*) or you could search online:

Amberley Signs
144 Frimley Green Road
Frimley Green
Camberley
Surrey GU16 6NA

Tel: 01252 836436
Website: **www.applegate.co.uk**

Driving School Supplies Ltd
2–4 Tame Road
Witton
Birmingham B6 7DS

Tel: 0121 328 6226
Website: **www.d-ss.co.uk**

ADI licence holders

ADI licences are supplied by the DSA in a clear, sticky, plastic holder. There are a couple of devices that enable you to fix them to the windscreen: a magnetic holder supplied by RCM Marketing (see above) or a gadget that relies on a suction cup and clip to fix the licence to the screen. This can be purchased from:

www.driving.org/mail-order.html (tel: 020 8665 5253)

Registering your business as a trade name

Business Link (**www.businesslink.gov.uk**)
Companies House (**www.companieshouse.gov.uk**)
Dupont (**www.dupont.co.uk**)
Start-ups (**www.startups.co.uk**)

Antivirus/spyware (software we use)

AVG (download for free and a very good product): **http://free.grisoft.com/**

Webroot (Spysweeper): **http://www.digitalriver.com/v2.0-img/operations/webroot/html/061108/webroot_4uk.html**

Ad-Aware: **http://www.lavasoft.com/single/search/adaware2007_plus.html**

Books and CD-ROMs for learners and ADI trainees

The Highway Code (DSA), *The DSA Theory Book for Car Drivers* (DSA), *Driving: The Essential Skills* (DSA), *Know Your Traffic Signs* (Department for Transport), *The Motor Car: Mechanical Principles* (DIA), *The Driving Instructor's Handbook* (Kogan Page), *The ADI Starter Pack Practice for Driving Instructors* (DSA), *The Official Theory Test for Car Drivers* (DSA), *The Hazard Perception Test* (CD-ROM, DSA) and other books/CD-ROMs can be purchase from bookshops, Halfords, Desk Top Driving (**www.desktopdriving.com**), HMSO (**www.tsoshop.co.uk/bookstore.asp?FO=1162833**) or Amazon (**www.amazon.co.uk**). Forms (including DVLA forms) are available from post offices.

Dual control suppliers

He-Man Dual Controls Ltd
Cable Street
Southampton SO14 5AR

Tel: 023 8022 6952
Website: **www.he-mandualcontrols.co.uk/**

Bestway
Unit 14
Abenglen Industrial Estate
Betam Road
Hayes
Middlesex UB3 1SS

Tel: 020 8581 6677
Website: **www.dualcontrols.com**

Other websites

Royal Society for the Prevention of Accidents (RoSPA): **www.rospa.com**

Institute of Advanced Motorists (IAM): **www.iamo.org.uk**

Cutting your telephone bills

Use the following link to cut the cost of calls on both landline and mobile phones: **www.18185.co.uk**. Charges could be as low as 0p per minute. With each call there is a small connection charge. Invoices are received via your email, and payment is automatically set up via a direct debit. We have had no problems with this service.

For other cheap phone call services and for many other ways to save money (e.g. bank accounts, 0% credit-card terms, etc.) you should consider registering for free at: **www.moneysavingexpert.com/tips/**. You receive weekly emails on all matters concerned with saving money. As a result of visiting this website, we decided to become a member of the Federation of Small Businesses (FSB **www.fsb.org.uk**) and then changed bank accounts to the Co-operative Bank. We no longer pay bank charges on any business account as long as we are in credit.

Career loans

You may be entitled to a career loan. This is a deferred repayment bank loan to help you pay for vocational training. Such loans are available through a partnership arrangement between the Department of Education and Employment and four major banks. The loan covers 80% of your course fee or 100% of your course fee if you have been unemployed for three months or more. It also covers related expenses (e.g. books, childcare, travelling expenses and any costs associated with disability). You can apply to borrow between £300 and £8,000 to pay for up to two years' training. For further information on this, contact the Career Development Loan Information Line: 0800 585 505. Alternatively, go to: **www.lifelonglearning.co.uk**.

Appendix 2
ADI training information

ADI grades

On completion of the Part 3 test, the candidate will be graded on their teaching abilities. Subsequently each ADI and trainer is given a periodic check test. The frequency of these tests (where an SE ADI observes a lesson or plays the part of a client) depends on the ADI's previous grade.

Grade 1 is the lowest grade, with Grade 6 being the highest. Grades 1–3 are a fail, which will mean that a candidate who has failed the Part 3 test must take another test. However, if Grades 1–3 are awarded on completion of a check test, there are further check-test opportunities where the ADI or the trainee ADI can show they have improved and so gain a Grade 4 or above.

Once fully qualified, an ADI Grade 4 should receive a check test every two years and Grades 5 or 6 every four years. There are currently discussions to link the grades with first-time test passes (i.e. the higher your first-time pass rate, the higher your grade).

ADI trainers

To find a list of ADI trainers near to you who have been registered on the Official Register of Driving Instructor Training (ORDIT), go to: **www.dsa.gov.uk**. Alternatively, order an ADI 14 starter pack either from the DSA's ADI branch on 0870 1214202 or from an ADI supplies website as advertised in any of the driving instructor magazines or on the websites given in this book. Remember, though, that there may be an ADI trainer near you who is good but who is not registered on the ORDIT. Talk to local instructors.

The Part 2 test: the practical driving test

☐ In order to take this test, your car must fulfil the following criteria, as specified by the DSA. It must:

☐ be a saloon car, hatchback or estate car properly taxed and insured and with a current MOT certificate, as necessary;

☐ be in good working condition with seat belts in working order;

☐ be capable of the normal performance of vehicles of its type (i.e. not have a temporary space-saver tyre fitted);

☐ be manual transmission, have right-hand steering and a readily adjustable seat with a head restraint for a forward-facing front passenger;

☐ have an adjustable interior rear-view mirror for the examiner's use; and

☐ not display L plates.

If the car has had a manufacturer's recall to rectify any problems, you may need the appropriate paperwork to prove this work has been carried out. Check for this at the DSA's website.

The Part 3 test: instructional ability (paired lessons – phases 1 and 2)

PST1

Phase 1: safety precautions on entering the car and explanation of the controls.
Phase 2: dealing with crossroads.

PST2

Phase 1: moving off and making normal stops.
Phase 2: overtaking, meeting and crossing the path of other road users, allowing adequate clearance, anticipation.

PST3

Phase 1: turning the vehicle round in the road to face the opposite direction using forward and reverse gears.
Phase 2: approaching road junctions – turning left and right.

PST4

Phase 1: reversing and reversing into a limited opening to the left or right.
Phase 2: emerging at road junctions.

PST5

Phase 1: how to make a controlled (emergency) stop, explanation/avoidance of three types of skid and practical instruction in the use of mirrors.
Phase 2: judgement of speed, making progress and general road positioning.

PST6

Phase 1: dealing with pedestrian crossings and the giving of signals in a clear and unmistakable manner.
Phase 2: parking close to the kerb using forward and reverse gears.

PST7

Phase 1: approaching junctions to turn either left or right.
Phase 2: dealing with pedestrian crossings and the giving of signals in a clear and unmistakable manner.

PST8

Phase 1: emerging at T-junctions.
Phase 2: overtaking, meeting and crossing the path of other road users, allowing adequate clearance, anticipation.

PST9

Phase 1: dealing with crossroads.
Phase 2: dealing with pedestrian crossings and the giving of signals in a clear and unmistakable manner.

PST10

Phase 1: overtaking, meeting and crossing the path of other road users, allowing adequate clearance, anticipation.
Phase 2: judgement of speed, making progress and general road positioning.

Resource material used on the Driving School Pro training courses

The Driving School Pro training courses use all the books listed in Appendix 1 for the ADI Part 1 test. Other materials are in a file (e.g. DVLA forms and DL25), together with a comprehensive set of notes regarding the qualities and attributes necessary to make a good ADI. The courses also cover the theory and practice of learning; teaching techniques and instructional techniques; the structure of lessons; and Q & A techniques. Tuition is also given on the skills needed to instruct (e.g. identifying, analysing and correcting errors; the manner of giving instruction; and maintaining professional relationships with clients).

Graphic Briefings are supplied (with accompanying notes) for all Part 3 lessons and lesson plans. Each trainee is provided with assessment records of every lesson delivered to their instructor in the role of learner driver client.

Booking the Part 1 theory test

Book your ADI Part 1 theory test online at **www.dsa.gov.uk** or telephone: 0870 01 01 372 (English) and follow the instructions (0870 01 06 372 for Welsh).

Appendix 3
Terminology used by examiners on the test

General directions

Throughout the drive continue ahead, unless traffic signs direct you other-wise, and when I want you to turn left or right I will tell you in plenty of time. Move off when you are ready, please.

Moving off and stopping

Would you pull up on the left at a convenient place, please.

or

Pull up along here, just before… please.

Drive on when you are ready, please.

Turning

Take the next road on the left/right, please.

Will you take the second road on the left/right, please.

At the end of the road turn left/right, please.

At the roundabout:

☐ turn left please (it is the first exit)

☐ follow the road ahead (it is the second exit)

☐ turn right please (it is the third exit).

Additional information will be given if necessary to assist the driver to plan their route through the hazard (examples are given above in brackets).

Emergency stop/controlled stop

Pull up on the left at a convenient place, please. Shortly I shall ask you to carry out an emergency stop. When I give this signal (simultaneously demonstrate and say 'Stop'), I'd like you to stop as quickly and as safely as possible. Before giving the signal I shall look round to make sure it is safe, but please wait for my signal before doing the exercise. Do you understand the instructions? Thank you. I will not ask you to do that exercise again. Drive on when you are ready.

Manoeuvres

Left-hand reverse: pull up along here just before you reach the next road on the left, please. I should like you to reverse into this road on the left. Drive past it and stop, then back in keeping reasonably close to the kerb.

Right-hand reverse: pull up on the left before you reach the next road on the right, please. I should like you to reverse into that road on the right. Continue driving on the left until you are past it then pull up on the right just past the junction, back in and continue well down the side road, keeping reasonably close to the right-hand kerb.

Reverse parking: would you pull up on the left well before you get to the next parked car, please. This is the reverse parking exercise. Would you drive forward and stop alongside the car ahead. Then reverse in and park reasonably close to and parallel with the kerb. Try to complete the exercise within about two car lengths.

Reverse parking (car park): this can be carried out at the beginning or the end of the test:

   □ Beginning of the test: would you pull forward either to the left or the right so that your wheels are straight, then reverse into a convenient parking bay. Finish within one of the bays.

   □ End of the test: I should like you to reverse park in the car park. Drive forward into the car park, then reverse into a convenient parking bay. Finish within one of the bays.

Turn in the road: would you pull up on the left just past the... please. I'd like you to turn your car around to face the opposite way, try not to touch the kerbs when you're turning.

Angle start: pull up on the left just before you get to the next parked car, please. (If necessary add: leave enough room to move away.)

Hill start: Use the 'normal stop' wording or specify the place.

Test routes

All the test routes in each test centre location can be found on the DSA's website (**www.dsa.gov.uk**). Look for details of your local test centre and/or enter keywords (e.g. test routes in Dorchester, Dorset).

Appendix 4
First-aid kits and accident books

Whether you think it is important to have a first-aid kit in the car is entirely your decision. Consider what would happen if you had a minor accident, though – do you need to clean a wound and do you have a plaster to cover it? What if your client injures themselves while in your care? Do you have an accident book? This should state what treatment was provided. What if you come across a road traffic incident? Could you offer any assistance? Do you have a first-aid qualification? Should you have a first-aid qualification?

Again, whether you have an accident book or whether you feel you should embark on a first-aid course is for you to decide. One of the authors of this book received several inquiries because he has a first-aid qualification. One client was a chronic asthmatic and carried a nebuliser around with her. He was asked if he knew how they worked and whether he was familiar with people who suffer from asthma. He answered positively to both for very valid reasons.

Remember, if you believe the situation you are facing is beyond your abilities, contact the relevant 999 service(s). Also, and sadly, there is always an element of risk if anyone other than a trained first-aider gives assistance. Where possible, you should have another person present when you come into bodily contact with the victim of an accident, especially if of the opposite sex.

First-aid kits

Our choice is the first listed. The Health and Safety Executive (HSE) recommendation is listed second. This is another choice for you to make:

Care4car
Commerce House
Telford Road
Bicester
Oxfordshire OX26 4LD

Tel: 0845 2252848
Website: **http://www.care4car.com/**

HSE kit in a box for the workplace (one-person travel kit)
First Aid Shop
24 Thomas Drive
Newport Pagnell
Bucks MK16 8TH

Tel: 01908 610093
Website: **www.firstaidshop.co.uk**

Accident report books

A health and safety accident report book is available from the First Aid Shop at the above address. This book complies with the Data Protection Act that states that personal details entered into accident books must remain confidential. Each page can be removed and stored in a secure location.

Appendix 5
Checklist for choosing your training car

First, use the following preliminary checklist for choosing your car:

- ☐ Price range and method of purchase?

- ☐ New or second hand?

- ☐ Approximate sale price of your old car?

- ☐ How much can you afford to pay for a new car?

Now create a shortlist of models and prices. Check the DSA's website for the suitability of each model. Look at ADI Internet forums for professional views on the cars being used by driving instructors. Check the European New Car Assessment Programme (NCAPY **www.euroncap.com**) safety rating. Consider the following:

- ☐ Reliability.

- ☐ Depreciation.

- ☐ The warranty.

- ☐ Security against theft.

- ☐ Can dual controls be fitted?

- ☐ Diesel or petrol?

- ☐ Colour.

- ☐ Not alloys.

- ☐ Fuel consumption figures.

- ☐ Three or five doors?

Checklist for the test drive

How do you find your ideal car? As mentioned earlier in this book, it is unlikely that you will find a car that measures up to all the criteria listed below, but the closer you get, the better it will be.

Take the car out on a test drive using learner driver territory such as housing estates, etc. Put the car through a simulated lesson. Drive it around sharp junctions. Go through the reversing exercises. Check out everything you would be expecting your clients to cope with. Try looking at the test drive through a learner's eyes rather than through your own experienced view. You will most likely be able to adapt and cope with a vehicle's shortcomings quickly – but will they?

During the static inspection ask the salesperson for some time on your own so that you can check the seats, instrument layout, position of controls, etc., without any pressure. Take your time and work down the list systematically.

Note: the following checklist is for new cars. If you are purchasing second hand you will obviously have to consider matters of wear and tear and the possibility of previous damage. If you doubt your mechanical knowledge we strongly advise that you take someone with you who definitely knows about cars or consider arranging for an AA or RAC inspection. Don't rush this purchase. Remember 'caveat emptor' ('let the purchaser beware').

So that you can have more than one copy of the checklist, remove the following pages then scan, copy and print.

Garage checklist

Date	
Name of garage or owner	
Make and year of car	
Recorded mileage	

Static inspection

Colour	
Diesel or petrol?	
Seats (are they well constructed, firm, supportive, fully adjustable and covered with a suitable material, with adequate space between driver and instructor?)	

Sounds of quality (there should be no squeaks and rattles. The doors should be well built with a good closing fit)	
Number of doors	
Storage space (the more the better)	
Instruments/controls (the instruments should be easy to see and the speedometer should be seen from the passenger seat. Control levers and knobs should be logical, sturdy and easy to use)	
Handbrake (this should be sturdy and located between the two front seats)	
Air conditioning (a real must, with good control over the internal environment. Also check this during the test drive)	
Mirrors (these should be large and electrically adjusted)	
Interior lighting (this must be adequate for instruction in the dark)	

Exterior light bulbs (ideally these should be easy to change)	
Boot space (is it adequate?)	
Not alloys	
Spare wheel (is this a normal-sized wheel or a space saver?)	
Servicing (what are the recommended intervals and costs?)	
Any evidence of servicing history (if second hand)?	
Warranty (what does this cover – over what time/miles?)	
Any finance deals?	
Any deals involving free dual controls, etc?	
Delivery time?	

Moving inspection

Clutch (this should be smooth, with a progressive bite-point which is at a reasonable height)	
Footbrake and gas pedal (these should be progressive and smooth)	
Driving in first and reverse gears (check the sensitivity of the gas pedal. Too sensitive may mean the learner will find it difficult/frightening)	
Foot pedals (these must be comfortably placed and not too close together)	
Steering (how does the steering wheel adjust? Powered steering? Small turning circle?)	
Gears (there should be no baulking and reverse must be easy to select)	
Windows (these must be a good size allowing a good view to the rear for reverse manoeuvres)	
Turbo charger (if fitted, this must ensure manageable acceleration)	
Engine management system (this should increase the speed at a reasonable and manageable rate)	
Air conditioning (how efficient is it?)	

Overall, on a scale of 1–5 (1 being poor and 5 being excellent), how did you rate:

☐ The car generally?

☐ The car as a training vehicle?

☐ The garage?

☐ The staff? Do you think you will receive a good, honest service from them over the next three to five years?

Initial price of new car   £_____

Final asking price of new car   £_____

Trade-in price of old car?   £_____

Final price of new car, minus trade-in allowance for old car   £_____

Cash value of any allowances (e.g. finance, dual controls, etc.) £_____

Appendix 6
Abbreviations

AA   Automobile Association

ABS   automatic braking system

ADI   approved driving instructor

APR   annual percentage rate

ASAP   as soon as possible

ATM   all time money (machine) or automated teller machine

BT   British Telecom

CD-ROM   compact disk read-only memory

CO_2 carbon dioxide

CRB   Criminal Records Bureau

DIA   Driving Instructor Association

DSA   Driving Standards Agency

DTP   desktop publishing

DVD   digital versatile disk

DVLA   Drivers and Vehicle Licensing Agency

EEA   European Economic Area

ETA   estimated time of arrival

EU   European Union

FSB   Federation of Small Businesses

H & S   health and safety

HSE   Health and Safety Executive

IAM   Institute of Advanced Motorists

IFA	independent financial adviser
MOAS	moving off and stopping
MOT	Ministry of Transport (test)
MP	member of Parliament
M-S-P-S/G-L	mirrors–signal–position–speed/gear–look
NCAP	(European) New Car Assessment Programme
PC	personal computer
PDI	probationary driving instructor
Q & A	question and answer
RAC	Royal Automobile Association
RoSPA	Royal Society for the Prevention of Accidents
RTA/I	road traffic accident/incident
SE	senior examiner
SEADI	senior examiner for approved driving instructors
URL	uniform resource locator (web addresses)
USB	universal serial bus

INDEX